NUTSHELLS

English Legal System

Titles in the Nutshell Series
A Level Law
Company Law
Constitutional and
Administrative Law
Consumer Law
Contract Law
Criminal Law
Employment Law
English Legal System
Environmental Law
Equity and Trusts
European Union Law
Evidence
Family Law
Human Rights
Intellectual Property Law
Land Law
Medical Law
Tort

Titles in the Nutcase Series
Constitutional and
Administrative Law
Contract Law
Criminal Law
Employment Law
Equity and Trusts
European Union Law
Human Rights
Land Law
Tort

YOU'VE GOT IT
CRACKED

NUT**SHELLS**

English Legal System

EIGHTH EDITION

by
PENNY DARBYSHIRE
Reader in Law
Kingston University

SWEET & MAXWELL

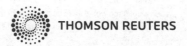 THOMSON REUTERS

First Edition – 1989
Second Edition – 1992
Third Edition – 1995
Fourth Edition – 1998
Fifth Edition – 2001
Sixth Edition – 2004
Seventh Edition – 2007

Published in 2010 by Thomson Reuters (Legal) Limited
(Registered in England & Wales, Company No 1679046.
Registered Office and address for service:
100 Avenue Road, London NW3 3PF)
trading as Sweet & Maxwell

*For further information on our products and services,
visit www.sweetandmaxwell.co.uk*

Typeset by LBJ Typesetting Ltd
Printed in Great Britain by Ashford Colour Press, Gosport, Hants

*No natural forests were destroyed to make this product;
only farmed timber was used and re-planted*

A CIP catalogue record for this book is available from the British Library.

ISBN: 978-0-414-04178-3

Contents

Using this Book

Welcome to our new look **NUTSHELLS** revision series. We have revamped and improved the existing design and layout and added new features, according to student feedback.

NEW DETAILED TABLE OF CONTENTS for easy navigation.

REDESIGNED TABLES OF CASES AND LEGISLATION for easy reference.

Table of Cases

NEW CHAPTER INTRODUCTIONS
to outline the key concepts covered
and condense complex and important
information.

INTRODUCTION

This chapter is about sources of law in Engla

- domestic legislation, including Acts
  legislation;
- European Union legislation;
- The European Convention on Human
- statutory interpretation;
- case law;
- custom;
- ~oks of authority; an⌐

**DIAGRAMS, FLOWCHARTS AND
OTHER DIAGRAMMATIC
REPRESENTATION** to clarify and
condense complex and important
information and breakup the text.

~U LAV.
are the players and wh.
their roles?

**Role of European Commission as
INITIATOR**

COR	European Parliament	ECOSOC
	First Reading	

COUNCIL OF MINISTERS

ouncil Approves   Council Does Not Approve

Adopts Common Pr

**END OF CHAPTER REVISION
CHECKLISTS** outlining what you
should now know and
understand.

Revision Checklist

You should now know and underst₃

- the sources of domestic law: ,
  Assembly Measures, Orders i
  especially bylaws and statut‹
  power, custom and books of

- the **European Conventior**
  applicable in the Engl'
  ~08:

END OF CHAPTER QUESTION AND ANSWER SECTION with advice on relating knowledge to examination performance, how to approach the question, how to structure the answer, the pitfalls (and how to avoid them!) and how to get the best marks.

…at information …
…ation is not repeated here.

QUESTION AND ANSWER

The Question

"While the common law is a very important so
sources of English law are growing in import

Advice and the Answer

…vice
…tion is a gift. It is a …

HANDY HINTS AND USEFUL WEBSITES —revision and examination tips and advice relating to the subject features at the end of the book, along with a list of Useful Websites.

HANDY HINTS

The golden rule for most law examinations w
all of the question (i.e. all its constituent par
(i.e. do not digress, keep your answer relevan
revision, practice and planning all have a role

Some issues may require discussion o
questions may involve breach of confidence i
also require consideration of passing off.

Preparation

…P examinations require ca…
…mat and st…

NEW COLOUR CODING throughout to help distinguish cases and legislation from the narrative. At the first mention, cases are highlighted in colour and italicised and legislation is highlighted in colour and emboldened.

…ove it to make a declaratic
…cts with the European Convention c
…ecial fast-track Parliamentary procedure to .
…eserving Parliamentary sovereignty.

Orders in Council
These are made by the executive government and have
not delegated, legislation: *R (Bancoult) v SS for Forei*
Affairs (No 2) [2008] UKHL 61 but they are reviewable
this does not offend against parliamentary supremacy

Welsh law
Under the **Government of Wales Act 2006**, th
…les, its legislature, can make, "Assembly Mea
…n its devolved competence, such as agric
…alth, transport, housing, local ·

Table of Cases

Table of Statutes

Introduction

....

WHAT IS THE ENGLISH LEGAL SYSTEM?

1. It is the domestic legal system of England and Wales, including courts and tribunals, procedure, legal services (legal aid) and the people operating the system—lawyers, judges, magistrates, magistrates' legal advisers, prosecutors, paralegals, jurors and tribunal members.
2. It is separate from the legal systems of Northern Ireland and Scotland. These three jurisdictions comprise the state, the United Kingdom. "Great Britain" comprises England, Wales and Scotland.

....

WHAT IS SPECIAL ABOUT THE ELS?

1. The ELS and English common law are among the oldest established legal systems and systems of law in the world.
2. English "common law" is so called because it was the ancient kings' law, applied commonly throughout the kingdom of England, replacing the customs and laws of the former kingdoms. England was a single kingdom by 1000. After the Norman invasion of 1066, the common law emerged in the twelfth century, because the Norman kings used the existing governmental infrastructure and their judges to spread the king's law, replacing the old Anglo-Saxon laws. (Baker, *An Introduction to English Legal History*, any edition, Butterworths, chapters 1 and 2).
3. "Common law" also means the system of legal principles developed by judges in the system of binding principle (precedent) and applied in later cases.
4. The ELS is the mother of all common law legal systems, worldwide, in Britain's ex-colonies and the Commonwealth. The common law world comprises the USA, Canada, Australia, New Zealand, the remainder of the Commonwealth and almost every country in which English is spoken. When the British established their empire across the globe, they spread the English language and English common law and procedure. The Scottish legal system and law are a hybrid between English common law and procedure and that of most of continental Europe, called the civil law.

THE WORLDWIDE SPREAD OF COMMON LAW

1. Because English law common law is ancient and stable and English judges have a reputation for being incorruptible, many foreigners and foreign states wish to have their disputes adjudicated according to English law, in London's Commercial Court, or by London arbitrators. It is very common for parties to specify in a contract that it is governed by English law and that any dispute arising will be determined according to English law. The City of London is an ancient centre for international trade, banking, insurance and commerce so its Commercial Court has been preeminent in establishing international law in these fields, including maritime law. Around 70 per cent of Commercial Court cases involve one foreign party, company or state and in 50 per cent of cases, both parties are foreign. London is also a springboard for the United States into Europe so London attracts large Anglo-American law firms. London is thus a very important legal centre, worldwide.

2. There is a two-way traffic in developing the common law. English common law principles and precedents form the historic basis of the law of contract, criminal law, tort (invented by English judges) and property throughout the common law world. When English judges cannot find a suitable precedent in English law to solve the problem before them, they look to the law reports of England's common law daughter jurisdictions to see how their judges have solved similar problems. These precedents are not binding on them but "persuasive". They may be persuaded to adopt the same reasoning and principles into English common law. Sometimes, English law has moved faster than the law in its common law daughters. American felonies and misdemeanours and the grand jury and the plaintiff bringing a civil case are English relics, disposed of and replaced in England and Wales in the twentieth century.

3. The Judicial Committee of the Privy Council, in London, acts as a supreme court for many common law countries who send their final appeals to be determined there. The judges sitting in this court are the UK Supreme Court justices. They are thus highly likely to apply the same principles while sitting in the two courts, thus English law and Commonwealth law develop in parallel. The decisions of the JCPC are persuasive but not binding precedents in English and Welsh courts.

4. The substantive law and procedure of England's common law daughters has generally remained astonishingly similar, so people qualified as lawyers in England and Wales find it very easy to re-qualify and practise in other common law countries and do not need to re-qualify in order to practise in some Commonwealth countries. Common lawyers can readily understand and apply one another's substantive law and procedure.

CHARACTERISTICS SHARED BY COMMON LAW COUNTRIES

Adversarial procedure
In civil and criminal cases, the judge is an unbiased umpire. It is up to the parties to bring all the information the court needs to adjudicate. They prepare the legal argument, they research and construct the argument and they present factual and technical evidence and witness testimony, unaided by the court. The court has no part in investigating the case. For example, common law countries do not have anything like the French examining magistrate or Scottish procurator fiscal empowered to direct police investigations in serious criminal cases.

Importance of common law, meaning judge-made law
Common law principles, made by judges, through the system of precedent, is just as important as statute law, codified law. Common law judges reason upwards from precedents not downwards from codes as judges do in civil law countries with codified law, such as France.

FURTHER READING

Darbyshire on the English Legal System, 9th edn, 2008, Sweet & Maxwell, and material cited and FURTHER READING listed therein

Sources of Law

INTRODUCTION

This chapter is about sources of law in England and Wales:

- domestic legislation, including Acts of Parliament and delegated legislation;
- European Union legislation;
- The European Convention on Human Rights;
- statutory interpretation;
- case law;
- custom;
- books of authority; and
- international law.

DOMESTIC LEGISLATION

Whilst most *principles* of English law are derived from common law and equity, the *details* are now contained in statute law, i.e. Acts of the UK Parliament and delegated legislation.

Acts of the UK Parliament

KEY POINT

Under the unwritten UK constitution, Parliament was given sovereign power by the **Act of Settlement 1700** but sovereignty is now qualified. Acts which run counter to European Community (EU) law may be suspended by the courts or declared invalid (*Factortame* (1991), see below). Otherwise, provided an Act has been passed by both Houses of Parliament, received Royal Assent and enrolled on to the parliamentary roll, it cannot be questioned by the courts. An exception to this is where the House of Lords (HL) refuses to pass a Bill. Under the **Parliament Acts 1911 and 1949**, it may be overridden and passed by the Commons only (e.g. the controversial **Hunting Act 2004**). Parliament cannot be bound by its predecessors or bind its successors.

The best source of information on how statute law is made is the UK Parliament website.

Functions of Acts

Revision of substantive rules of law

Since 1965, the Law Commission has helped keep the law under review and modernisation and simplification have sometimes been prompted by its reports or those of ad hoc Royal Commissions, or individuals, such as those of Leggatt on tribunals and Auld LJ on criminal procedure.

Consolidation of enactments

Where law has evolved piecemeal, a single replacement Act can be passed without debate.

Codification

The enacting of rules of common law.

Collection of revenue

The annual Finance Act(s) implement the budget.

Social legislation

This broad category covers the many facets of the Government's running of the country and organisation of society. It is often the subject of party political differences.

Forms of Acts

There is a distinction between (the more common) public Acts which are of general effect, and private Acts, which deal with personal or local matters. Procedure differs. Distinguish between Government Bills (the vast majority), private Bills, hybrid Bills and private members' Bills, promoted by M.P.s or peers, selected by ballot. Matters of conscience (e.g. abortion) are often left by the Government to be dealt with in this way.

Validity of Acts

Parliamentary sovereignty precludes the courts' questioning Acts of Parliament where there is no conflict with Union law. The UK has no written constitution against which the courts could test their constitutionality, as does the Supreme

Court in the US. An attempt was made to challenge the validity of the **Hunting Act 2004** in 2005 but it was rejected by nine law lords: *R. (on the application of Jackson) v AG* [2005] UKHL 56. The Human Rights Act 1998 permits the High Court and those above it to make a declaration of incompatibility, where they find an Act conflicts with the European Convention on Human Rights 1950. This triggers a special fast-track Parliamentary procedure to amend the offending Act, thus preserving Parliamentary sovereignty.

Orders in Council
These are made by the executive government and have been held to be primary, not delegated, legislation: *R (Bancoult) v SS for Foreign and Commonwealth Affairs (No 2)* [2008] UKHL 61 but they are reviewable by the courts, because this does not offend against parliamentary supremacy.

Welsh law
Under the Government of Wales Act 2006, the National Assembly for Wales, its legislature, can make, "Assembly Measures" in relation to matters within its devolved competence, such as agriculture, education, the environment, health, transport, housing, local government, sport and the Welsh language.

Delegated legislation
Most delegated legislation takes the form of statutory instruments: rules and orders. Parliament has delegated power to other law-makers, mainly government ministers, in various Acts of Parliament. Most statute law consists of statutory instruments rather than Acts. There were 3,327 in 2008 but only 33 Act. Most European Community law comes into the UK via these. Parliament also delegates law-making powers to public bodies and local government to pass laws within their own field or locality, in the form of byelaws.

EUROPEAN UNION LEGISLATION

Sources
The European Communities Act 1972 (ECA 1972) provides that any UK enactment has effect subject to existing "enforceable Community rights" so, by implication, parliamentary sovereignty is limited to passing legislation which does not conflict with EU (Community) law. EU treaties are its primary source of law. They are binding on the EU institutions and Member States and, in certain circumstances, may create individual rights enforceable in national courts. The fundamental Treaty is the Treaty of Rome 1957. Article 249 of the EC Treaty (EC), now art.288 of the Treaty on the Functioning of the EU, sets out the following secondary legislative provisions:

Regulations have general, binding and direct applicability in all Member States.

Directives are binding, as to results to be achieved, upon each Member State to whom they are addressed, but leave form and methods to each Member State.

Decisions are binding on those to whom they are addressed.

Applicability and enforcement

Distinguish between *direct applicability* and *direct effect*. The former concept refers to the fact that all Treaty Articles and all Regulations immediately become part of the law of each Member State. The latter concept is the vehicle through which individuals may assert that, under Community legislation, they have rights which the European Court of Justice (ECJ) will protect and upon which they can rely in national courts. The question as to whether a piece of legislation has direct effect is determined thus:

Treaty Articles

In the *Van Gend en Loos* case [1963] E.C.R. 1, the plaintiffs needed to know if they could rely on old art.12 EC to ignore the Dutch Government's increase of import duty. The ECJ, on a reference from the Dutch tribunal, held they could. The Article created individual enforceable rights because:

- it was clear;
- it was unconditional; and
- its implementation required no further legislation in Member States so that Member States were not left with any real discretion.

These tests have been applied to test the direct effectiveness of Treaty provisions.

Regulations

These have immediate applicability, as part of the law of each Member State. There is no need for further legislation to implement them and they are binding in their entirety and, like Treaty Articles, can be directly effective according to the above criteria.

Directives

The same criteria have been applied to give *direct effect* to unimplemented Directives, where a person can show that they would have been granted a right under the Directive and they suffered a loss as a result of non-implementation. This only works, however, where they are acting against the State (and, as above, the provision is clear, precise, unconditional and leaves no room for discretion in implementation). The principle of direct effect cannot be implemented against a private party so there is no such thing as horizontal direct effect, confirmed in *Faccini Dori* [1995] All E.R. (EC) 1. Nevertheless, Directives have an *indirect effect* in that national law may have to be reinterpreted to conform to them. The *Marleasing* case [1990] E.C.R. I-4135 held that national courts were bound by old art.5 EC to reconcile all national law, pre- or post-dating a Directive, in conformity with it. This development has mitigated the results of the lack of horizontal direct effect. In *Francovich and Bonifaci v Italy* [1991] E.C.R. I-5357, the ECJ decided that an individual could sue the state directly where he had suffered loss as a result of non-implementation of a Directive by the Member State.

Decisions

The ECJ has held that these may create individual rights which domestic courts must protect. They have direct applicability and may have direct effect.

Supremacy of Community law

KEY POINT

Under Community law, that law takes precedence over any earlier or later domestic law. In *Costa v ENEL* [1964] E.C.R. 585, the ECJ ruled that, in creating a Community with its own legal capacity, "the member states have limited their sovereign rights, albeit within limited fields, and have thus created a body of law which binds both their nationals and themselves". **The European Communities Act 1972 (ECA),** s.2 gives effect to Community law (EU law) in the UK. Section 3(1) directs the UK courts to have regard to Community law. This includes the principle of supremacy. Where it appears to the English courts that there is inadvertently conflicting English legislation, they will endeavour to give effect to EU law.

The *Factortame* cases of 1990–91 (on Spanish fishing in UK waters) illustrate the power and significance of EU law. In 1990, on a reference for a preliminary ruling from the House of Lords (law lords), the ECJ opined that a UK court could suspend the application of any Act of Parliament on the grounds of its perceived incompatibility with Community law and that Community law gave the national court the power to grant such interim relief, even though no such power existed in (English) national law. Acting on this reference, the House confirmed that an interim injunction could be granted against the Crown, in such exceptional circumstances, to restrain it from enforcing an Act which, on the face of it, contravened Community law. The novelty here was the use of an injunction against the Crown since this was, otherwise, impossible.

Subsequently, in 1991, the ECJ indeed ruled that part of the Merchant Shipping Act 1988 ran counter to the EC Treaty. The concept of an Act of Parliament's being declared not to be in conformity with Community law came as no news to lawyers in the UK, who were swift to point out that we gave up part of our sovereignty in the ECA 1972, but media reaction was scandalised.

Cross-border co-operation and harmonisation of domestic law and procedure

As a result of a 2002 Decision, a European arrest warrant is now effective. In 2004, the European Commission laid down certain minimum rights in criminal procedure. The jurisdiction of the ECJ to rule on matters like this, which are not part of Community law but agreed within the Justice and Home Affairs pillar of the EU, varies from state to state. In the UK, the ECJ has no such power. The ECJ has always had power to interpret and rule on the validity of Community law but in 2005, it ruled, rather alarmingly, that it has jurisdiction to rule on the validity and interpretation of European Union law, i.e. law made in the two outer "pillars" of the EU, not just the central pillar, which is the Community. The ECJ's powers in these respects are now set out in arts 275 and 276 of the Treaty on the Functioning of the EU.

In 2006, an agreement was reached to use a harmonised procedure in cross-border small claims. This was a matter of agreement between the Member States, not a matter of Community law. A European code of contract has been under development since 1982.

THE EUROPEAN CONVENTION ON HUMAN RIGHTS 1950

KEY POINT

The Convention is a Treaty of the Council of Europe NOT an EU Treaty. It preceded the EU and has been ratified by a bigger group of states (46).

It was drafted by UK lawyers after World War II to protect basic freedoms and was incorporated into English law by the **Human Rights Act 1998**, s.1. Its articles, as incorporated, are as follows.

1. Obligation to respect human rights.
2. Right to life.
3. Prohibition of torture.
4. Prohibition of slavery and forced labour.
5. Right to liberty and security.
6. Right to a fair trial.

7. No punishment without law.
8. Right to respect for private and family life.
9. Freedom of thought, conscience and religion.
10. Freedom of expression.
11. Freedom of assembly and association.
12. Right to marry.
13. Right to an effective remedy.
14. Prohibition of discrimination.
15. Restrictions on political activity of aliens.
16. Prohibition of abuse of rights.
17. Limitation on use of restrictions on rights.

- Some rights are absolute, such as art.3. Some admit exceptions, such as art.2 and most are subject to restrictions to ensure respect for other rights and freedoms.
- The **Human Rights Act 1998** s.2 provides that when a court or tribunal is determining a question in connection with a Convention right, it "must take into account" judgments, decisions or declarations of the European Court of Human Rights, or opinions or decisions of the Commission or the Committee of Ministers.
- Section 3 says: "(s)o far as possible, primary legislation and subordinate legislation must be read and given effect in a way which is compatible with the Convention rights".
- Section 6 makes it unlawful for any public authority, including any court or tribunal, to act in a way incompatible with a Convention right.
- Any party to legal proceedings can rely on a Convention right. Whether the Convention confers horizontal rights (citizen against citizen) is, however, ambiguous because while the interpretation obligation binds all of us, ss.6 and 7 only allow challenges to actions of public authorities.

KEY POINT

Note the wording of s.3. Whereas EU law takes sovereign precedence over UK law, Convention law does not, because of this "let out" clause. There is no obligation on the courts, nor do they have the power, to disapply a domestic Act but they are obliged to reinterpret legislation to comply "where possible". If not, the High Court and above can make a declaration of incompatibility, under s.4(2).

This has occurred a number of times. For instance, in April 2003, the HL, in *Bellinger v Bellinger* [2003] UKHL 23 declared that the non-recognition of gender reassignment, in English law, for the purposes of allowing a transsexual to marry, was incompatible with arts 8 and 12. Section 11 of the **1998 Act** provides for a fast-track legislative procedure so delegated legislation can amend offending primary legislation but this was not done in response to *Bellinger*. Instead, the Government introduced the Gender Recognition Bill (now Act) in 2003.

STATUTORY INTERPRETATION

The need for interpretation

Interpretation of statutes is necessary because Parliament can only be expected to provide a broad legal framework. It cannot spell out how an Act will apply in practice, in every set of circumstances which may arise in future. Bennion, in his book *Bennion on Statute Law* (Longman, 1990) identified several factors which can cause doubt as to statutory meaning:

- Ellipsis: the deliberate omission of words the draftsman thinks are implied. This causes no problem provided all the statute's readers realise what is implied.
- Broad terms: where the draftsman uses generic terms, deliberately leaving the decision as to what falls into that category to the judge or statute user. For example, does the word "vehicle" cover a child's tricycle and a donkey cart?
- Politic uncertainty: where ambiguous words may be used deliberately, where a provision is politically controversial or the Government lacks clear intent.
- Unforeseeable developments: where novel circumstances arise after the passing of an Act.
- Miscellaneous drafting errors: including accidental ambiguity and even printing errors.

In *R v Chambers* [2008] EWCA Crim 2467, the CA realised that for seven years no-one had noticed that the law on confiscating smuggled tobacco had changed so over 1,000 confiscation orders were flawed. The CA said this was symptomatic of a wider problem that the law was inaccessible to everyone today, because most of it was secondary legislation; the volume of legislation had increased; legislation could not be found in a single place; and there was no comprehensive statute law database.

Traditional "rules" of statutory interpretation

The judges do not employ strict rules of interpretation but common approaches have been identified and labelled as such. To a certain extent, judges select which "rule" to use in accordance with the result they seek to achieve in the case before them.

The literal rule

This simple approach involves giving words their ordinary, plain, natural meaning. Sometimes judges feel defeated by the clear words of a statute from reaching a decision that they and the public consider just. An example of this occurred when Diane Blood was refused consent to use her dead husband's sperm, because of the lack of his written consent, as required by the Human Fertilisation and Embryology Act 1990: *R. v Human Fertilisation and Embryology Authority Ex p. Blood* [1996] 3 W.L.R. 1176.

The golden rule

Rather than sanction an absurdity by a literal interpretation, judges sometimes depart from giving words their "ordinary natural meaning". If words have more than one meaning, the least absurd is to be applied.

The mischief rule

This rule is commonly described as the last judicial approach, if the first two "rules" fail to assist interpretation. It is a much wider approach than the two and concentrates on determining the meaning of words by discovering the aim of the statute, the "mischief" at which the statute was directed. Under the contextual approach, described below, the aim of the statute is considered as part of the context of the words being interpreted. Many modern judges take this approach from the outset.

The contextual approach

Sir Rupert Cross in *Statutory Interpretation* (Butterworths, 1976 and later editions) described this judicial approach to statutory interpretation.

Considering the context

In giving words their ordinary or technical meaning or in delimiting broad terms, the judge must take them in their general context within the statute, and in the statute's external context. According to *Attorney General v Prince Ernest Augustus of Hanover* [1957] A.C. 436 ("the *Hanover* case") this includes the rest of the statute, the preamble, the existing state of the law and the factual context, i.e. the problem that the statute was intended to remedy. The statute must be read as a whole. Some judges refer to "a purposive approach", aiming to promote the general legislative purpose of a statute, to avoid, for example, ambiguities which would defeat its purpose, but this can only be done where judges can determine this from internal or external aids to interpretation (see below) and where such an approach is not defeated by presumptions of interpretation. An example of a contextual approach was *Laroche v Spirit of Adventure* [2009] EWCA Civ 12, the CA held that a hot air balloon was an "aircraft" according to the *Pocket Oxford Dictionary* but the plain, ordinary meaning was not necessarily determinative. On a purposive construction of the Carriage by Air Acts (Application of Provisions) Order 1967, it was reasonable to suppose that Parliament intended such balloons to be included, as they were capable of being used for international transport.

Strict construction of criminal law
Penal statute law is construed strictly. The CA held there was no canon of statutory construction which empowered any court to write into a statute words which were not there, on the grounds that Parliament ought to have enacted a provision which it had not: *R. v Morgan R. v Bygrave* [2008] EWCA Crim 1323.

Modifying statutory language to avoid unreasonableness
Under this approach, the judge may read in words which are necessarily implied and he has a limited power to add to, alter or ignore statutory words, to prevent a provision from being unintelligible, absurd, unreasonable, unworkable or totally irreconcilable with the rest of the statute, or to prevent a conflict with Community law or the **European Convention on Human Rights 1950**. According to case law, this approach should only rarely be necessary if, for example, there is a mistake in drafting leading to an anomaly. There are a number of cases where the words "and" and "or" have been interchanged, to make sense of the statute. This approach was taken in *Inco Europe v First Choice Distribution* [2000] 1 W.L.R. 586 but the law lords warned that the purpose of the statute must be abundantly clear.

Rules of language
Ejusdem generis   means a general word following a list of particular ones will normally be construed as restricted in scope to applying to things or persons of the same class (genus) as those listed, e.g. in *Powell v Kempton Park Racecourse Co* [1899] A.C. 143 it had to be decided whether "house, office, room or other place" included Tattersall's ring at the racecourse. It was held not to be included because "house, office, room" created a genus of indoor places so an outdoor racecourse could not fall within an "other place".

Noscitur a sociis   means a word is to be construed as being similar to the rest of the objects in a list.

Expressio unius exclusio alterus   means that a specified member of a class impliedly excludes other members. For example, the inclusion of "coal mines" in this list: "lands, houses, tithes and coal mines" has been held to impliedly exclude other mines.

Internal aids to interpretation
The first resort in interpretation may be found in the wording of the statute itself.

* Other enacting words. Another section may provide a clue to interpretation and there is often an interpretation section. For example, the Access to Justice Act 1999 defines such phrases as "criminal proceedings".
* Long title. This sets out the aims of the Act. It can be as short as two lines, if the Act has one topic, or as long as a page, in a statute with diverse aims. Some Acts now contain an "overview", as does the Income Tax (Earnings and Pensions) Act 2003, s.1.
* Preamble. Some Acts, such as the Courts and Legal Services Act 1990, set out their purpose more clearly in a section. The preamble cannot prevail over clear enacting words.
* Short title, such as Banking Act 2009
* Headings, side notes and punctuation. Although not voted on by Parliament, these are acceptable aids.

External aids
* Historical setting of the statute.
* Dictionaries and textbooks.
* Past practice.
* Related statutes.
* Previous statutes. Consolidating statutes are presumed not to alter the law but clear language may rebut this.
* Subordinate legislation.
* Government publications (with certain qualifications), e.g. Royal Commission or Law Commission reports and Government White Papers, in which the Government sets out the policy behind legislation. Many statutes are now issued with explanatory notes. They appear alongside the Act on the OPSI website.
* Treaties and international conventions.
* Parliamentary materials. Until 1993, judges declined to refer to *Hansard*, the report of Parliamentary proceedings, but in *Pepper v Hart* [1993] A.C. 593 the House of Lords (HL) held that this rule should be relaxed where legislation was ambiguous or obscure, or the literal meaning led to an absurdity and, in identifying the true intention of the legislature, judges could be assisted by clear statements by the Bill's promoter. This principle has been applied more widely than intended. This was considered and criticised by the HL in *R. v Secretary of State for the Environment, Transport*

and the Regions Ex p. Spath Holme Ltd. [2001] 2 A.C. 349. Nevertheless, in *Wilson v First County Trust (No.2)* [2003] UKHL 40, the House extended the principle to decisions on compatibility with the **European Convention on Human Rights.**

Presumptions

General principles, such as the principles of natural justice and the principle that no one should be allowed to profit from their own crime, override even the clearest language. Presumptions, however, can be ousted by clear words: Parliament must spell out any intention to avoid the following presumptions:

- against changing the common law;
- against ousting the jurisdiction of the courts. The judges guard their own powers jealously and even some of the clearest "ouster" clauses have been held not to preclude judicial review;
- against interference with vested rights and freedoms (fundamental human rights) and that property cannot be taken away without compensation;
- against unduly penalising the citizen so criminal liability must be based on fault, unless clearly stated, and any penalty must be clear;
- against retrospective applicability;
- that statutes do not bind the Crown so that a very common inclusion in an Act is a section specifically binding the Crown (e.g. the Royal family are not exempted from liability for traffic offences); and
- that Parliament does not intend to contravene the UK's international (Treaty) obligations, including the **European Convention on Human Rights,** the EU treaties and so on.

The interpretation of EU law

The most important key to interpretation of EU law is the approach of the European Court of Justice. The ECJ is more concerned with examining purpose and context than wording. The Treaties are drafted in general terms, leaving it to the EU institutions, through secondary legislation, to fill in the details. The ECJ can review the legality of acts and omissions of EU institutions. The ECJ takes a dynamic approach in favour of the aims of the Union and the supremacy of EU law over national law, for example giving direct effect to Directives. The ECJ employs a "rule of effectiveness" which means that preference should be given to the construction which gives a rule its fullest effect and it takes a contextual approach, referring to the general scheme of the Treaty or other Treaty provisions. Exceptions to EU rules and Treaty obligations are restrictively interpreted. For example, the principle of free movement of workers is limited by public policy, public security and public health and these limitations are strictly construed.

The ECJ refers to "general principles of law", common to all Member States, derived from national law and the principles laid down by the European Court of Human Rights, which can be employed in the interpretation of Treaty provisions but which cannot override them. These principles include such things as proportionality, fair hearing, equality and legal certainty. The general principles of law are an important source of EU law and are used to interpret EU Treaties and when examining national law for conformity with the Treaties, as well as being almost a free standing source of law.

CASE LAW (PRECEDENT)

Significance

Much substantive law in the English legal system is a creation of the judiciary, through the application and development of case law and precedent. For example, the bulk of the law of tort and contract, as well as important crimes such as murder and common assault, are a creation of the judges and not of Parliament. This distinguishes the English legal system from the codified systems of Europe and elsewhere. Under the system of binding precedent or *stare decisis* (meaning "to stand by previous decisions"), the lower courts are bound to apply the legal principles set down by the senior courts in earlier cases. This provides consistency and predictability and obviously depends on a system of law reporting. The part of a case which forms the binding precedent is:

- a statement of law (as opposed to fact);
- which forms part of the *ratio decidendi* (reason for the decision); and
- in a court whose decisions are binding.

The *ratio decidendi*

The *ratio decidendi* (plural, *rationes decidendi*) has been defined by Sir Rupert Cross, in *Precedent in English Law* (Clarendon, 1961), thus:

> "any rule of law expressly or impliedly treated by the judge as a necessary step in reaching his conclusion, having regard to the line of reasoning adopted by him, or a necessary part of his direction to the jury".

The *ratio decidendi* (*ratio*) must be distinguished from an *obiter dictum* (plural, *dicta*) which is a statement of law not necessary for the decision in the case. A judge may decline or find it difficult to apply the *ratio decidendi* of a previous decision because:

- he does not agree with it and has managed to find discrepancies in the instant case which allow him to distinguish it from the precedent; or
- no statements of principle appear in the precedent; or
- the *ratio* is difficult to extrapolate because different sets of reasoning have been used to found one decision, e.g. in HL cases where there appear to be up to five *rationes decidendi* (e.g. *Hyam v DPP* [1975] A.C. 55; *Boys v Chaplin* [1969] 2 All E.R. 1085).

The function of the court hierarchy in the system of precedent

The European Court of Justice and the European Court of Human Rights

Under s.3 (1) of the **European Communities Act 1972**, decisions of this court are binding in matters of Community law, EU law on all courts up to and including the UKSC. Under s.2 of the **Human Rights Act 1998**, all courts must "take into account" the case law of the European Court of Human Rights, the European Commission and Committee of Ministers when determining whether a Convention right has been breached.

The UK Supreme Court (formerly House of Lords)

Decisions of the UKSC/HL are binding on all the courts below it and, until 1966, were binding on later decisions of the House itself. In 1966, however, the Lords of Appeal (law lords) announced that they no longer intended to be bound by their previous decisions. This new, self-conferred power was intended to be used sparingly, however, to cater for revisions in law necessitated by changing social circumstances. It was such a change in societal attitudes which, arguably, led to the first application of the new power, in *British Railways Board v Herrington* [1972] A.C. 877, strengthening tortious protection for child trespassers, when the harsh precedent of *Addie v Dumbreck* [1929] A.C. 358 was overturned. Since then, the House has used this power or consciously declined to use it, on a number of occasions. In 2003, the House used its power to overrule the *Caldwell* definition of recklessness, in *R. v G* [2003] UKHL 50. In 2006, it used this power in *Horton v Sadler* [2006] UKHL 27, to rule that a court has a wide power to disapply a statutory time-limit in a personal injury action. In *R (on the application of Purdy) v DPP* [2009] UKHL 45 they ruled that art. 8(1) of the E Conv HR was engaged, when a terminally ill person sought assisted suicide, departing from their previous decision in *R on the application of Pretty v DPP* [2002] 1 All ER and instead following the ECtHR in *Pretty v UK* (2346/02) [2002] 2 FCR 97.

The Court of Appeal (Civil Division)

The CA is bound by HL or UKSC decisions and its decisions are binding on all those courts below it.

Young v Bristol Aeroplane Company Ltd [1944] K.B. 718

The CA held itself to be bound by its own previous decisions, with three exceptions:

1. Decisions given *per incuriam* (through lack of care). This refers to decisions made in ignorance or forgetfulness of some statutory provision or some binding precedent, notably because it has not been brought to the court's attention.
2. Conflicting decisions of the CA. There is no consensus on which of two conflicting decisions, the earlier or the later, should be followed.
3. Decisions impliedly overruled by the HL, now UKSC. Later case law added the following exception.
4. Decisions on interlocutory appeals, i.e. decisions taken by a Court of Appeal of only two judges.

Smith, Bailey & Gunn on the Modern English Legal System (Sweet & Maxwell see latest edition) lists, in addition, the following possible exceptions to *Young v Bristol Aeroplane*:

5. Inconsistency with an earlier HL decision: the HL (or UKSC) decision is binding.
6. Inconsistency with a Privy Council decision. This, however, is a dubious creation of Lord Denning M.R.
7. Inconsistency with international law. International law must be followed.
8. Where the CA is the court of last resort, with no appeal available to the HL/UKSC.
9. The HL in *Davis v Johnson* [1979] A.C. 264 reaffirmed the rule that, other than in these cases, the CA is bound by its own previous decisions. (See also *Rickards v Rickards* [1990] Fam. 194.

The Court of Appeal (Criminal Division)

This division is bound by the UKSC (formerly HL), by itself and by its historic predecessors, unless it is a CA decision falling into one of the exceptions in *Young v Bristol Aeroplane*. Further, the CA said in *R. v Spencer* [1987] A.C. 128 that, where they were dealing with the liberty of the subject, they would depart from authority in the interests of justice to the appellant. Sometimes the CA regrets being bound by the House of Lords/UKSC where the law clearly needs reforming and Parliament has not spared the time to do so: *A v Hoare* [2006] EWCA Civ 395. A "full court" of five Lords Justices has the power to overrule a previous decision of a court of three and full courts have been used regularly in recent years. It is uncertain whether the two divisions of the CA bind each other but in some instances they have manifested an intention not to be so bound, for example, in their conflicting approach towards the constitutionality of jury vetting in *R. v Sheffield Crown Court Ex p. Brownlow* [1980] Q.B. 530 and *R. v Mason* [1980] 3 W.L.R. 617.

The High Court

It is bound by the CA and HL/UKSC but is not bound by other HC decisions.

Divisional Courts of the High Court

Divisional Courts of the HC are, when exercising their appellate function, binding on their successors and amenable to the principles in *Young v Bristol Aeroplane* but not when exercising their judicial review function: *R. v Greater Manchester Coroner Ex p. Tal* [1984] Q.B. 67.

The Crown Court, magistrates' courts and county courts

These decisions are seldom reported and are not binding on any court.

Tribunals

Upper Tribunal decisions are binding on the chambers below them.

Persuasive precedents

Precedents which are not binding may be taken as persuasive and, indeed, have played a significant part in assisting judicial creativity where there are gaps in the law, a classic example being the development of liability for negligent misstatements resulting in pure economic loss, from an *obiter* statement of the HL. The following precedents are persuasive:

1. *Obiter dicta* of the HL/UKSC.
2. Decisions of the Privy Council. In a unique decision, *R. v James, R. v Karimi* [2005] EWCA Crim 14 the Court of Appeal decided to follow a PC decision instead of an earlier HL decision. The PC had decided in *R. v Holley* [2005] UKPC 23, an appeal from Jersey, that the HL precedent on provocation in murder, *R. v Smith (Morgan)* [2001] 1 A.C. 146 had been wrongly decided.

The CA chose to follow the PC decision, predicting that, if it did not, the HL (comprised of the same judges as the PC) would overrule it.

3. Decisions from other common law jurisdictions.
4. Textbooks.
5. Judgments of parallel courts, where these are not binding, for example, the High Court.

PREROGATIVE POWER

This type of power is a residue of the power formally exercised by the monarch. It is normally exercised by ministers. It is not trivial or obscure. It includes such important matters as the conduct of foreign relations and the power to wage war and peace. Because these powers are historic and not prescribed in writing, their vagueness is perceived by critics as undesirable, as it is solely defined by the courts and then only when its use is challenged. When a statute is passed on the same topic as a prerogative power, the courts assume that the Act has superseded the prerogative power.

CUSTOM

The common law of England was formed from the customary laws of Anglo-Saxon kingdoms. Custom rarely plays a part in modern England and Wales, except where the court is prepared to accept evidence of established custom, as a defence. It sometimes helps develop elements of international commercial law, however, such as banking.

BOOKS OF AUTHORITY

Modern, authoritative, well-established textbooks, such as Smith & Hogan's *Criminal Law* and practitioner texts such as *Archbold* on criminal law and procedure are often relied on as dependable statements of the law, because of the expertise of those who wrote them. Similarly, ancient books of authority are occasionally cited.

INTERNATIONAL LAW

Private international law covers private relations, such as family affairs. Public international law governs relations between states. It becomes binding in English law when the UK government signs and then ratifies the treaty that has created it. The courts take a purposive approach to construction. International law, where the UK is a contracting party, overrides domestic common law.

Revision Checklist

You should now know and understand:

- the sources of domestic law: Acts of the UK Parliament, Welsh Assembly Measures, Orders in Council, delegated legislation, especially bylaws and statutory instruments, case law, prerogative power, custom and books of authority;

- the **European Convention on Human Rights** and how it was made applicable in the English and Welsh courts by the **Human Rights Act 1998**;

- European Community law (EU law) and the mechanism by which it was and is incorporated into UK law, as prescribed in the **European Communities Act 1972**;

- the concept of sovereignty of the UK Parliament and how this is subordinate to the sovereignty of EU law;

- the hierarchy of precedent and the way precedent works;

- the approach judges take in interpreting statute law, using rules and presumptions, internal and external aids and context; and

- the different statutory powers and interpretive approaches of the courts in EU law and Convention law, remembering that the latter preserves UK Parliamentary sovereignty and remembering that the European Convention is not a Treaty of the EU.

FURTHER READING/UPDATING

Darbyshire on the ELS, 2008, material cited and FURTHER READING listed therein and website updates and the Sweet & Maxwell website.
C. Manchester and D. Salter, *Exploring the Law* (latest edn)
Statute Law Review
Times law reports

Websites
Council of Europe
Europa
Francis Bennion
National Assembly for Wales
OPSI for statute law but amended statute law is on *Lexis* and *Westlaw*.
UK Parliament: excellent, informative website and naturally, one cannot better
its factual information on the legislative process, which is why the infor-
mation is not repeated here.

QUESTION AND ANSWER

The Question

"While the common law is a very important source of law, the many other
sources of English law are growing in importance".

Advice and the Answer

Advice
This question is a gift. It is a very straightforward test of knowledge of the
sources of law but it does require some though to evaluate the
IMPORTANCE of the common law now, relative to all the other sources.

Answer guide
1. Explain what common law is. Historically, it meant the law prom-
   ulgated by the royal courts in Westminster and commonly applied
   throughout the kingdom of England, from around the Norman
   Conquest, distinct from canon law (church law) and the local
   systems of customary law from the tiny historic kingdoms from
   which England was formed. Nowadays, common law means law
   developed and applied by judges on a case by case basis, in the
   system of precedent.
2. Briefly explain how judges develop common law principles
   through precedent.
3. Give examples of judge-made common law, commenting on their
   importance, because the question requires an evaluation of
   importance. Obvious examples are the basic rules of contract,
   the whole of the law of tort and common law crimes, such as

murder. You can draw on your knowledge of important modern cases. For example, the law lords have been very outspoken about torture and reminding us of the common law hostility to torture in their judgments from 2005.

4. Mention that judge-made common law is important as a source of law not just in England and Wales but throughout the common law world because English common law has formed the base of substantive law and procedure, not just in England, but in all her common law daughter jurisdictions. Also, briefly explain how common law principles are developed on a worldwide basis.

5. Then turn to the other sources of law. The more common law is replaced by codified law—statutes, statutory instruments, international treaties and European Union law, the more it retreats into the background and diminishes in importance.

6. You can visit the OPSI website and explain how many Acts and statutory instruments are made each year and see how many more there are now than decades earlier.

7. Having said that, judge-made law is still much more important in common law countries than European civil law jurisdictions because the base of their law are principles embodied in codes, whereas our principles are articulated and developed by judges in the system of binding precedent.

8. Remember to explain and evaluate the importance of all the sources of law explained in this chapter.

9. EU law is very important indeed, since 1972/3 because it is sovereign over all domestic law and the ambit of the EC then EU has expanded since then, covering more areas of our lives. Examine the wording of the 1972 Act and the relevant judgments of the ECJ to show that the concept of sovereignty of EU law derives from both domestic law and EU law.

10. The European Convention on HR has been recognised since the 1950s, when the UK ratified the Convention but grown in importance very significantly since our courts were empowered to enforce it from 2000, by dint of the 1998 Act. Give practical examples of its influence on our domestic law but it is also well worth pointing out that the content of the articles is clearly derived from common law rules (e.g. see chapter on criminal procedure). UK lawyers drafted the Convention and so took the principles from common law and the Convention is now applied in 46 contracting

states so it has had an extremely important indirect influence, which is hardly ever acknowledged.

11. Remember to explain the importance of statutory interpretation and, briefly, the principles and presumptions of SI.

12. Do not forget to assess the importance of international law. London is a major international centre. With globalisation, international law takes on a greater importance.

13. Explain the modern significance of prerogative power. Historically it was of major importance because it was power exercised by the monarch. Although Acts of Parliament supersede the prerogative, prerogative power is not obscure, or merely historic. It governs the whole of foreign relations, such as declarations of war and peace.

14. Mention that while custom was very important in the development of the common law, it is far less important now, though it does play a part in the development of international law.

15. Reach a brief conclusion based on what you have just argued.

Figure 1

THE COURT STRUCTURE

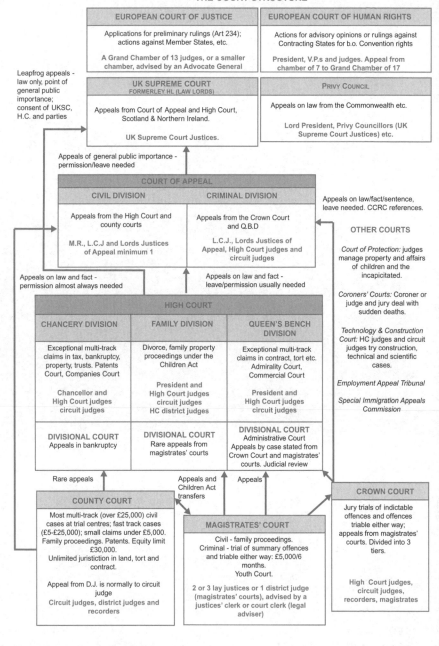

Leapfrog appeals - law only, point of general public importance; consent of UKSC, H.C. and parties

EUROPEAN COURT OF JUSTICE

Applications for preliminary rulings (Art 234); actions against Member States, etc.

A Grand Chamber of 13 judges, or a smaller chamber, advised by an Advocate General

EUROPEAN COURT OF HUMAN RIGHTS

Actions for advisory opinions or rulings against Contracting States for b.o. Convention rights

President, V.P.s and judges. Appeal from chamber of 7 to Grand Chamber of 17

UK SUPREME COURT
FORMERLEY HL (LAW LORDS)

Appeals from Court of Appeal and High Court, Scotland & Northern Ireland.

UK Supreme Court Justices.

PRIVY COUNCIL

Appeals on law from the Commonwealth etc.

Lord President, Privy Councillors (UK Supreme Court Justices) etc.

Appeals of general public importance - permission/leave needed

COURT OF APPEAL

CIVIL DIVISION

Appeals from the High Court and county courts

M.R., L.C.J and Lords Justices of Appeal minimum 1

CRIMINAL DIVISION

Appeals from the Crown Court and Q.B.D

L.C.J., Lords Justices of Appeal, High Court judges and circuit judges

Appeals on law/fact/sentence, leave needed. CCRC references.

OTHER COURTS

Court of Protection: judges manage property and affairs of children and the incapicitated.

Coroners' Courts: Coroner or judge and jury deal with sudden deaths.

Technology & Construction Court: HC judges and circuit judges try construction, technical and scientific cases.

Employment Appeal Tribunal

Special Immigration Appeals Commission

Appeals on law and fact - permission almost always needed

Appeals on law and fact - leave/permission usually needed

HIGH COURT

CHANCERY DIVISION

Exceptional multi-track claims in tax, bankruptcy, property, trusts. Patents Court, Companies Court

Chancellor and High Court judges circuit judges

FAMILY DIVISION

Divorce, family property proceedings under the Children Act

President and High Court judges circuit judges HC district judges

QUEEN'S BENCH DIVISION

Exceptional multi-track claims in contract, tort etc. Admirality Court, Commercial Court

President and High Court judges circuit judges

DIVISIONAL COURT
Appeals in bankruptcy

DIVISIONAL COURT
Rare appeals from magistrates' courts

DIVISIONAL COURT
Administrative Court Appeals by case stated from Crown Court and magistrates' courts. Judicial review

Rare appeals

Appeals and Children Act transfers

Appeals

COUNTY COURT

Most multi-track (over £25,000) civil cases at trial centres; fast track cases (£5-£25,000); small claims under £5,000. Family proceedings. Patents. Equity limit £30,000.
Unlimited jurisdiction in land, tort and contract.

Appeal from D.J. is normally to circuit judge
Circuit judges, district judges and recorders

MAGISTRATES' COURT

Civil - family proceedings.
Criminal - trial of summary offences and triable either way: £5,000/6 months.
Youth Court.

2 or 3 lay justices or 1 district judge (magistrates' courts), advised by a justices' clerk or court clerk (legal adviser)

CROWN COURT

Jury trials of indictable offences and offences triable either way; appeals from magistrates' courts. Divided into 3 tiers.

High Court judges, circuit judges, recorders, magistrates

The Court Structure

INTRODUCTION

> **KEY BACKGROUND POINTS**
>
> - It is not a coherent, logically developed "system". It grew piecemeal because the history of the ELS is such a long one.
> - The distribution of work between courts and tribunals is somewhat arbitrary but has not been questioned until recently, in the Leggatt Report (2001).
> - We seldom question whether we need two criminal and two civil courts of first instance (trial courts). Auld LJ did so in the Criminal Courts Review.
> - Most civil cases are settled out of court, by negotiation, or dealt with by ADR, or arbitration, or allocated by statute to a tribunal.
> - Most criminal acts committed by young people (and some by adults) result in a caution and, increasingly, offences are dealt with by fixed penalty.
> - Most civil cases were shifted down into county courts, following **The Courts and Legal Services Act 1990,** reserving the High Court for complex, important or specialist cases.
> - Criminal cases have progressively shifted down into the magistrates' courts over the last three centuries.

CRIMINAL COURTS

Magistrates' courts

These are the most important criminal courts because they dispose of around 95 per cent of criminal business. In Outer London and the provinces, most cases are heard by unrobed lay justices (lay magistrates), sitting in twos or threes, advised by a justices' clerk or court clerk, known as a legal adviser. In Inner London, most cases are heard by a professional district judge (magistrates' courts) (DJMC).

Of these criminal cases, many are *summary* traffic offences, most of which are decided in the absence of the defendant, who may plead guilty by post.

Another quarter are *triable either way* offences, cases of median seriousness, where the defendant has the option of a Crown Court appearance instead. The rest are other summary offences. Magistrates hear almost all cases against young people aged 10–17, in private, in the youth court. (Some are heard in the Crown Court, as explained in the criminal procedure chapter). There are over 29,000 unpaid lay magistrates, who sit part-time in around 365 courts in England and Wales, and 136 professional magistrates, DJMCs. In 2009, virtual courts are being piloted, trying the defendant on a video link from the police station and, if he pleads guilty, sentencing him where possible.

Criticisms

- It is an accident of history that most cases are dealt with in Inner London by a DJMC, often advised by a professionally qualified clerk, yet in Outer London and the provinces, the same work is mainly done by lay justices whose legal advisers are not always barristers or solicitors.
- Although most criminal business is heard in magistrates' courts, Parliament and the senior judiciary often make the mistake of developing the law as if most criminal cases were still heard by judge and jury in the Crown Court.

Community Justice Centres

The first was opened in 2004, in Liverpool, copying an American project. There are now ten more. Local people help select the judge (usually a circuit judge). The CJC has the jurisdiction of a magistrates' court and is meant to involve the local community in tackling crime and anti-social behaviour. One theme is restorative justice.

Drugs Courts

By 2009, there are six of these special magistrates' courts. Offenders convicted of low level crime can be sent for sentencing.

The Crown Court

This is the criminal court of first instance which deals with the most serious (*indictable*) offences, as well as some *either way* offences. It hears appeals from magistrates' courts. It replaced assizes and quarter sessions, following the Courts Act 1971. There is one single Crown Court, divided between 92 centres in six circuits, in three tiers:

First tier

High Court (HC) judges deal with the most serious offences, as well as some civil HC cases.

Second tier

HC judges may sit.

Third tier

HC judges do not normally visit.

Most work is handled by circuit judges. Recorders (part-timers) may sit in all tiers. If there is a trial, guilt is determined by a jury of 12. Appeals are heard by a judge and two lay magistrates.

KEY POINT

There are three basic categories of criminal case:

- Summary (least serious), heard in the magistrates' court.
- Triable either way (either way) heard in the magistrates' court or Crown Court.
- Indictable (most serious), heard in the Crown Court.

There is a fourth category, summary triable on indictment but you need to remember the basic three.

The Queen's Bench Division of the High Court (QBD)

Its Divisional Court, with two or three judges, hears *appeals by way of case stated* from the magistrates' court and the Crown Court (except in relation to CC trials) and, in the Administrative Court, it exercises *supervisory jurisdiction* over certain matters in the Crown Court and magistrates' courts, i.e. judicially reviewing the legality of their proceedings and orders.

The Court of Appeal (Criminal Division)

This is presided over by the Lord Chief Justice (L.C.J.) and its Vice-President. It normally comprises one Lord Justice (there are 37) and two HC judges. Important appeals are heard by five judges. Certain circuit judges are authorised ("ticketed") to sit. It hears appeals on fact, law and sentence. Appeals against sentence may be heard by two judges. It normally sits in the Royal Courts of Justice in the Strand, London but has sat in Cardiff, Liverpool and elsewhere.

The UK Supreme Court (UKSC), formerly House of Lords Appellate Committee

It was created in October 2009 by the Constitutional Reform Act 2005, in Parliament Square, in order to enhance the constitutional separation of powers, replacing the *law lords* who were, historically, a committee of the House of Lords. It hears *points of law of general public importance*, including civil appeals from Scotland and civil and criminal appeals from Northern Ireland, and there are always two Justices from Scotland and one from NI. The minimum number of Justices determining an appeal is three but normally five, or up to nine hear important cases. As well as the 12 fulltime Justices, acting judges may be drawn from senior judges or retired Justices or law lords. The Court may be assisted by specially qualified advisers.

Background

In 2003, the Department for Constitutional Affairs proposed the replacement of the HL Appellate Committee with a Supreme Court and, after much debate, this was achieved in the 2005 Act. The Government was keen to remove obvious breaches of the separation of powers (executive/legislature/judiciary). It considered that judicial independence, required by art.6 of the **European Convention on Human Rights 1950**, necessitated removing the historic link of the law lords (judiciary) to Parliament (legislature) and this argument had been made repeatedly by two law lords, Lords Bingham and Steyn. Lord Chancellor Falconer was keen to emphasise that there was no intention to create a court like the US Supreme Court, with a power to overturn legislation. The court does the same work as the law lords and most of the first Justices were law lords. Additionally, it has been given the jurisdiction over devolution cases formerly exercised by the Judicial Committee of the Privy Council. Those who opposed this reform, such as Lord Mackay, expressed concern that the law lords would lose their valuable right to speak in Parliament, debating proposed legislation.

The Judicial Committee of the Privy Council (JCPC)

It moved from Downing Street to the UKSC building in October 2009. It hears appeals from some Commonwealth countries, including republics. It also hears appeals from some ancient courts and church courts. It comprises the Lord President of the Council, UKSC Justices, former Privy Councillors who have held high judicial office, and Privy Councillors who hold or have held high judicial office in the Commonwealth. Normally, a board of five sits.

Criticism

Commentators here and abroad suggested the JCPC's jurisdiction in death penalty appeals from the Caribbean was inappropriate for modern, European judges and their views often conflicted with those of the inhabitants of islands from which appeals are sent. For instance, in 2006, it abolished the mandatory death penalty in the Bahamas: *Bowe v The Queen* [2006] UKPC 10. Human rights Q.C., Keir Starmer said this was the culmination of a 10-year litigation strategy to abolish the death penalty in the Caribbean. For this reason, some Caribbean countries have created their own Court of Justice.

The European Court of Justice (ECJ)

It sits in Luxembourg and consists of 27 judges, one from each EU state. The most important cases are heard by a Grand Chamber of 13. One peculiar feature, unknown to English law, is the function of the Advocates General. One A.G. sits with the bench in each hearing and may question the parties, delivering an opinion some weeks later. This sets out facts, law and a suggested judgment. There is a European Court of First Instance, to be renamed the General Court. Its current jurisdiction is on its website.

The ECJ hears:

- applications from Member States' courts for preliminary rulings on EU law;
- actions against Member States for failure to fulfil obligations under EU law;
- actions for annulment of EU regulations, directives or decisions;
- review actions for EU institutions' failure to act; and
- appeals on points of law from the Court of First Instance and certain reviews.

For detail see its website.

The European Court of Human Rights (ECtHR)

KEY POINT

This court is NOT an institution of the EU and should not be confused with the ECJ, above.

It sits in Strasbourg and enforces states' obligations under the **European Convention on Human Rights 1950** for those 46 *contracting states* which have ratified this treaty, including the UK. The UK has been taken before the court on many occasions, necessitating amendments in domestic law. It has 46 judges, one from each state. They sit in chambers of seven or, for important cases and appeals from a chamber decision, a Grand Chamber of 17.

CIVIL COURTS

> **KEY POINT**
>
> Civil, non-family cases, if defended, are allocated to one of three tracks:
>
> - small claims, under £5,000, heard by district judges at the county court;
> - fast track, under £25,000, heard by DJs or circuit judges in the county court; or
> - multi-track, heard by DJs or CJs or HC judges, in county court trial centres, or district registries of the HC, or in the HC in London.

Civil courts include the UKSC, the JCPC, the ECJ and the ECtHR, as described above.

Magistrates' courts

They have a significant civil case load, predominantly in the Family Proceedings Court. Lay justices who hear family cases are selected from specially trained panels. DJMCs may sit alone. All are empowered to make and enforce most orders ancillary to a divorce, such as money orders. Under the Children Act 1989, they have the same powers over children as the HC and county courts so they can make residence and contact orders, and so on.

County courts

These are the most important courts for most people involved in a civil case as they handle most civil business. They were created in 1846, as a cheaper, simpler, local alternative to the HC. There are now 218. Their jurisdiction is set out in the **Courts and Legal Services Act 1990** and delegated legislation. It consists of cases on contract, tort, property, divorce and other family matters, bankruptcy, admiralty, equity, probate, race relations, etc. Many cases are debt claims. Solicitors have rights of audience in all cases. Most cases are managed or heard by county court district judges, others by circuit judges or recorders. All types of judge sit alone, except in rare trials where liability is determined by a jury. Some big courts have been renamed *civil justice centres* because they also offer ADR (alternative dispute resolution).

The High Court

It sits in the Royal Courts of Justice (Strand) and also at various centres in the six circuits.

The Queen's Bench Division

This is the largest, generalist division, consisting of the President of the QBD and 74 HC judges. It deals with common law (tort and contract) and actions for recovery of land and property. It contains two specialist courts, Admiralty and Commercial, and it administers the Technology and Construction Court. It sits in London and many district registries, at county courts. The Divisional Court of the QBD hears some appeals from the magistrates' courts and the Crown Court and exercises the supervisory jurisdiction, judicially reviewing the legality of the actions of the inferior courts and, in the Administrative Court, public bodies such as central and local government. The AC hears planning appeals. Outside the Divisional Court, all HC judges sit alone, except in rare tort cases, where they may sit with a jury.

The Chancery Division

This consists of the Chancellor of the HC and 16 HC judges. It hears claims relating to property, trusts, wills, partnerships, revenue, contentious probate, company and personal insolvency, intellectual property and copyright. It includes two specialist courts, Patent and Companies. It sits in London and in eight provincial centres. Its Divisional Court hears bankruptcy and insolvency appeals. Some appeals have shifted to the Finance and Tax Chamber of the Upper Tribunal in 2009, which is staffed by Chancery Division judges.

The Family Division

This consists of the President of the Family Division and 19 HC judges, who hear divorce cases and ancillary matters and **Children Act** cases in London and many district registries at county courts. There are 20 HC district judges who sit at the Principal Registry of the Family Division in Holborn, London, not to be confused with county court district judges.

Other Elements of the High Court

Some tribunals are also superior courts of record, part of the HC, such as the Employment Appeal Tribunal.

The Court of Appeal (Civil Division)

It hears appeals on fact and law from the HC and county courts. It is headed by the Master of the Rolls, who is Head of Civil Justice. Lords Justices of Appeal may sit alone, or in pairs or threes, or fives, dependent on the seriousness of the appeal. It sits in the RCJ and occasionally in Cardiff.

COURT MANAGEMENT

The Ministry of Justice runs the courts and legal services. The Justice Secretary, a Cabinet minister, is also the Lord Chancellor (in 2009 an M.P., though the L.C.

may be from the House of Lords). He is assisted by junior ministers. They develop policy and promote and make relevant legislation, and the Justice Secretary is answerable to Parliament. Her Majesty's Courts Service, an independent government agency, created by the Courts Act 2003, administers the courts on a day-to-day basis. Local policy is determined by 42 local courts boards, of judges, magistrates and local people, created by the **Courts Act 2003**. Judges are constantly concerned that the courts budget is continually reduced, in real terms, and the present government has a new policy that the civil courts should pay for themselves. They have increased civil court fees significantly. Judges consider that the courts should be provided as a public (social) service, as they are in other countries.

OPEN COURTS

Courts should be open to the public, under art.6 of the **European Convention on Human Rights,** with certain exceptions, such as national security, children and family privacy. Until 2009, access to family courts was extremely patchy and confusing. Some family proceedings are now open, if permitted by the judge, and may be reported, again with restrictions as imposed by the court. Although the UKSC may and will broadcast proceedings, under the **Constitutional Reform Act 2005,** other courts may not be photographed or broadcast. Though televising other courts was considered in 2004–05, this will not proceed because the current Justice Secretary, Jack Straw, is opposed to it.

COURT RESTRUCTURING

The distribution of work between criminal courts was considered by the James Committee in 1976. Consequently, some crimes were downgraded as *either way* or *summary*, thus shifting work down into the magistrates' court. Lord Justice Auld, in the Criminal Courts Review 2001, suggested a three-tier criminal court but this was not adopted by government. Lord Mackay L.C. saw the **Children Act 1989** as a first step towards the creation of a unified family court but little progress has been made, except for unified rules, despite the fact that family courts exist in many other common law countries. The distribution of civil cases was considered by the *Civil Justice Review* 1988, which resulted in the **Courts and Legal Services Act 1990,** which shifted most civil business down to the county court. The L.C. announced a proposal to create a single civil court and a single family court, following consultation in 2005, but this has come to nothing. A 2009 report by Sir Henry Brooke concluded negatively.

With the help of the court structure diagram, you should now know and understand:

- the courts of England and Wales and how they relate to the European Court of Human Rights, the European Court of Justice and the UKSC;

- the distribution of civil and criminal work, in outline;

- which judges sit in which courts; and

- why the UKSC was created and how it differs from the law lords.

FURTHER READING/UPDATING

Darbyshire on the ELS, 2008, Chapters 6 and 7 and website updates.
Court structure diagram, in this book
HM Courts Service website for court addresses—and some courts have their own websites, such as the Old Bailey, the UKSC and the Privy Council
ECJ and ECtHR website
Criminal Courts Review 2001
Civil Justice Review 1988

QUESTION AND ANSWER

The Question

"The English court structure is not a faultlessly coherent, logical system". Discuss.

Advice and the Answer

Advice
1. Read the general guidance at the back of this book.
2. Study the court structure diagram and the chapters on civil and criminal procedure, as they are also relevant to answering this question.

3. Read much more widely than this book, which provides only skeleton information.

4. Obviously, there are arguments both ways on this point, otherwise this point would not have been raised for discussion.

Answer guide

1. Introducing your answer, explain that the court structure is very old and has been continually developing since before 1066 so it cannot be expected to be as faultlessly coherent as a newly-designed court structure might be expected to be.

2. Examine the ways in which it *is* coherent. Generally speaking, it is fairly clear which cases are heard in which courts. It is fairly logical, with two civil courts of first instance and two criminal courts of first instance. Generally, business is distributed between them sensibly, thanks to successive reforms (name the James Committee and the Civil Justice Review), with the lower, cheaper courts handling most business, in fairly swift procedures, heard by with unpaid lay magistrates and lowest ranking judges, district judges. The HC is reserved for unusually complex or expensive civil cases and the Crown Court handles serious crime. Appeals are heard at an appropriate level (especially since reform of civil appeals in 1999, as explained in the civil procedure chapter), with the very top court being reserved for cases of points of law of general public importance. There are specialist courts with knowledgeable judges for cases requiring expertise, such as the Commercial Court and the Technology and Construction Court.

3. Progressive piecemeal reforms, like the redistribution of civil and criminal cases and the creation of the UKSC (explain why and how), have made the system more logical and coherent.

4. Nevertheless, there are deficiencies in coherence and logic.

   a. Family cases, especially children cases, may start in one of three courts and often, parents whose relationship is breaking up may need to appear in two or three types of court, which is very confusing, stressful and time consuming, as well as expensive to the taxpayer. The promised family court has never arrived.

   b. As for the civil courts, it might be more sensible to have one civil court, as considered by the Civil Justice Review 1988 and again recently, scrapping the division between county court and HC and scrapping the HC divisions. This would allow for more fluid distribution of work. Different ranks of judges could be retained, with work allocated to them according to its seriousness and complexity. Under the present system, many HC cases in the provinces are heard by "ticketed" circuit judges, demonstrating a considerable overlap and the falsity of the present HC/county court distinction.

c. In the criminal courts, many trivial "either way" cases are heard in the expensive Crown Court, because we are one of very few countries who give the defendant the choice of trial court so he can choose jury trial for stealing a bottle of milk. While the right to jury trial is very important to the English and Welsh, it is very expensive.

d. On the other hand, unlike our common law daughter jurisdictions in North America, we do not allow the defendant to choose to be tried by judge alone in the Crown Court, instead of judge and jury. Auld L.J. found that in Canada and the USA, many defendants opted for judge-alone trials. This would be much cheaper than jury trial and why deny the defendant the choice?

e. There is no logic in who adjudicates in magistrates' courts. London's preference for professional magistrates (DJMCs) is an accident of history. Again, the defendant has no choice between a bench of three lay justices and a professional judge, because the court allocates the cases. Also, if we value collective decision making on guilt and innocence and thus use 12 jurors or three magistrates, why do we allow any cases to be determined by a single DJMC?

f. While the civil appeal structure was reformed in the **Access to Justice Act 1999** so that an appropriate court and judge is used for each case, the criminal appeal structure is confusing, illogical and in need of reform, as demonstrated in a recent Law Commission paper.

g. The distribution of business between tribunals and civil courts is somewhat arbitrary, as the Leggatt review of tribunals commented.

5. Brief, concluding remarks, summarising the answer.

Civil Procedure

....

4

INTRODUCTION

1.   Procedure in common law countries is *adversarial*, meaning it is up to the parties to prepare their case, researching and presenting relevant evidence and legal argument, unaided by the court. The judge is a neutral, non-interfering umpire.

2.   The civil degree of proof is *on the balance of probabilities*, much lower than the criminal degree, *proof beyond reasonable doubt*, so the court merely decides whether the claimant's case is more plausible than the defendant's case.

3.   Generally, the claimant's aim is to satisfy the judge of the defendant's liability.

4.   The state provides the civil courts to enable claimants to make use of the civil law against parties who have committed a civil wrong or threaten a civil wrong against them, such as a tort or breach of contract.

5.   Unlike criminal cases, the state as a whole has no interest in the outcome, though elements of the state may be sued, such as a health authority.

6.   Most civil disputes (well over 90 per cent) are settled between the parties or their solicitors, by negotiation.

7.   In the exceptional case, where the aggrieved party goes to court, most civil cases are heard in the county court by a district judge or, much less likely, a circuit judge. The High Court is reserved for special cases.

8.   Trial is by judge alone, with rare exceptions where a jury is used to determine liability and damages. Some civil cases are heard in the magistrates' court and thus determined by lay magistrates or a district judge (magistrates' court).

9.   In this chapter we examine:

   •   the Civil Procedure Rules (CPR) 1998, brought in as part of the "Woolf reforms";
   •   their background;
   •   evaluations of their success; and
   •   a description of the civil appeal procedure.

We also look at the procedure for referring a point of European Union law to the European Court of Justice, in a civil or criminal case. *Note* the *trial* process, both civil and criminal, is examined in the chapter on criminal procedure.

....

CIVIL LITIGATION FROM 1999, FOLLOWING THE WOOLF REFORMS

The **CPR 1998** replaced two sets of rules for the High Court and county court, in April 1999. They, and the Practice Directions (not law) accompanying them, embodied a radically different approach to civil procedure from the Dickensian litigation preceding them and were modelled on recommendations by Lord Woolf in *Access to Justice* (1996) better known as the Woolf Report.

Civil Procedure Act 1997
Section 1 provides for one set of practice rules. Section 1(3) requires "that the civil justice system is accessible, fair and efficient". Section 2 provides for a Civil Court Rule Committee to include people "with experience in and knowledge of" consumer affairs and lay advice. Section 6 established a Civil Justice Council comprising the Master of the Rolls (head of civil justice and of the Court of Appeal (Civil Division)), judges, lawyers and consumer/lay advice and litigant representatives, to keep the civil justice system under review, advise the Lord Chancellor (the minister in charge of the courts) and suggest research.

KEY POINT

In the debate on the **Civil Procedure Bill,** this quotation from Lord Woolf illustrates a frustration shared by many critics of the old system, long identified as being in need of reform:

"When I set out on the inquiry which resulted in my report, I was very conscious that since 1885 there had already been over 60 reports, each urging reform of the civil justice system, yet the situation on which I had to report was one which many commentators described as being in crisis".

The Civil Procedure Rules 1998
The *overriding objective* is set out in r.1.1 (paraphrased):
> The rules enable the court to deal with a case justly:

a.   ensuring the parties are on an *equal footing*
b.   *saving expense*
c.   dealing with the case in a way which is *proportionate*

to the amount of money involved
to the importance of the case
to the complexity of the issues
to the financial position of parties.

d.   ensuring that it is dealt with *expeditiously* and *fairly* and allotting to it an
       appropriate share of the court's *resources*.

e.   The court *must* apply the objective in interpreting the rules and exercising
       their powers. (My emphasis).

Pre-action protocols

These are statements of best practice in negotiation, encouraging exchange of
information and putting the parties into a position to settle fairly. If they are
ignored, the judge can punish the uncooperative party in costs, once the case
comes to court. The pre-action stage is important, because most people settle
their civil disputes by negotiation. In 2009, a new **Practice Direction** (not law)
on pre-action behaviour attempted to strengthen the effects of protocols (Useful
explanation at (2009) 159 N.L.J. 151 by A. Wadey): The PD tries to help parties
to settle so that proceedings do not have to be issued. It encourages early
exchange of information and ADR. Parties MUST, for example,

- exchange info in reasonable time;
- disclose relevant documents;
- consider minimising cost of experts; and
- ATTEMPT ADR (though cannot be forced to do so).

KEY POINT

From 2009, as a matter of practice (not law), the court MUST take account
of compliance with this PD and pre-action protocols when making
directions.

Starting proceedings

The claimant (formerly plaintiff) or court issues and serves the claim on the
defendant. This must include particulars of the claim (statement of case) or
they must be served within four months. They may include points of law, witness lists and documents, and must include statements of truth and value and
specify the remedy sought.

The defendant must, within 14 days:

- admit the claim;
- file a defence (statement of case); or
- acknowledge.

If not, the claimant may request a *default judgment* (Pt 12). This means asking the court to grant his claim as the defendant has not entered a defence. *Most cases end at this point.* The defendant may issue a claim against a co-defendant or third party or make a *counterclaim* (Pt 20). The claimant may reply and defend. The parties may write direct to others requesting further information.

Allocation

Defended claims (i.e. the exceptions) are allocated to one of three tracks, once the defendant has completed the pre-trial checklist.

- Small claims track for most actions under £5,000, except housing possession and personal injury, where the limit is £1,000. Higher value claims may be allocated to this track by consent.
- Fast track for most cases £5–25,000, which can be tried in a day. (Until April 2009, the limit was £15,000). Oral expert evidence is limited to two fields and one expert per field.
- Multi-track for claims over £25,000 or over one day's trial.

Claims with no monetary value are allocated where the judge considers they will be dealt with most justly. The judge may transfer a case to another court.

Discretionary factors

The procedural judge must have regard to:

- the nature of the remedy sought;
- the complexity of facts, law and evidence;
- the number of parties;
- the value of the counterclaim;
- whether there will be oral evidence;
- the importance of the claim to non-parties;
- the parties' views; and
- the circumstances of the parties.

The Woolf Report suggested the following cases for the multi-track:

- those of public importance;
- test cases;
- medical negligence cases (now "clinical disputes"); and
- cases with the right to jury trial.

District judges (DJs) have unlimited jurisdiction to assess damages, unless otherwise directed.

The court's duty to manage cases

This had already been introduced from 1994 in Practice Directions, including timetabling, the requirement for skeleton arguments and limitation of oral argument. The *duty* now includes:

- encouraging parties to co-operate;
- identifying issues at an early stage;
- deciding promptly which issues can be disposed of summarily;
- deciding the order of issues;
- encouraging Alternative Dispute Resolution (ADR);
- helping parties settle;
- fixing timetables;
- considering cost benefit (of every element of the case);
- grouping issues;
- dealing with a case in the absence of one or more parties;
- making use of IT; and
- directing the trial process quickly and efficiently.

Sanctions for failure to comply include striking out, costs and debarring part of a case or evidence. Trials will only be postponed as a last resort. Most cases of all types are managed by county court DJs. HC masters manage most cases in the Royal Courts of Justice, except commercial cases. The court controls what evidence it is prepared to hear and the format in which it is prepared to hear witnesses.

Interim orders

The parties may apply for the orders listed below. This should be less necessary than before 1999, because of case management: the court may act on its own initiative. There is an obligation to apply early. Hearings may be by telephone.

- Pre-action remedies if urgent;
- applications without notice (formerly called *ex parte*);
- extensions or shortening of time;
- requiring attendance;
- separating or consolidating or excluding issues;
- deciding the order of issues;
- staying (pausing) all or part of the case, hoping for settlement;
- interim injunctions/declarations;
- freezing injunctions and search orders;
- pre-action disclosure (formerly discovery) or inspection; and
- interim payments and payments into court.

Summary judgment

This may be initiated by the claimant, defendant or court, where the claim or defence *"has no real prospect of success"*. The court may enter judgment, dismiss the case, strike out a claim, or make a conditional order.

Expert witnesses

Lord Woolf felt that over-use of experts had made litigation costly and unduly adversarial. The assumption now is that one witness will suffice or, if more than one is permitted, that they will agree a statement pre-trial. Under Pt 35, their duty is to help the court and no party may call an expert or use a report without the court's permission. In fast-track trials where an advocate is briefed, the court cannot normally order costs for a solicitor to accompany her.

Small claims procedure

Hearings are in public (as required by the **European Convention on Human Rights 1950**) but are normally held in the DJ's chambers. She may adopt any procedure she considers fair, including hearing lay representatives. Appeal lies to a circuit judge on law or serious irregularity. Costs are fixed at low levels.

Fast-track procedure

The intention is for the court to maintain *proportionality*, which means limiting the costs recoverable from the unsuccessful party. The aim is to increase access to justice by removing uncertainty and obtaining a speedy result. The court directs the timetable and fixes the trial date no more than 30 weeks ahead. The intention is to provide little scope for either party to create extra work to gain a tactical advantage. Lord Woolf said it was important for the court to protect the weaker party against oppressive or unreasonable behaviour by a powerful party.

Standard directions now include disclosure, the exchange of witness statements, expert evidence, and fixing the trial date. Parties are encouraged to use a single expert, or a court-appointed expert. The standard timetable is nine months from the issue of proceedings to trial. An indexed, paginated document bundle must be produced to the court three to seven days pre-trial and may include an agreed case summary. The judge is meant to pre-read the bundle. Trial costs are meant to be kept *proportionate* to the amount recovered. Other costs are assessed summarily by the judge after the trial.

Multi-track procedure

This varies. Simple cases are treated like fast track ones. Complex ones may have several directions hearings:

- a case management conference attended or dealt with by telephone, by lawyers familiar with the case, which may require a case summary;

- a pre-trial review of the statement of issues; and
- other directions hearings.

Disclosure
This was formerly known as discovery. Lord Woolf thought uncontrolled discovery was a major generator of cost. Now, standard disclosure requires only documents on which a party relies and documents which:

- adversely affect his case;
- adversely affect another party's case;
- support another party's case; and
- are required by a Practice Direction.

The court's power to control evidence
The court has power to control the delivery of evidence and whether it is prepared to hear oral, hearsay, or written evidence, etc.

Offers to settle (Part 36)
This procedure encourages the parties to settle by financial incentive. Under the old rules the defendant could make a payment into court and force the plaintiff to take a gamble: take the money or proceed to trial and risk paying both sides' costs since the time of the payment in. The intention of the new rules is that allowing the claimant to make an offer to settle alters the balance of power. The judge knows nothing of the offer to settle.

Wasted costs
The court may make a wasted costs order against a representative if he has acted improperly, unreasonably or negligently and his conduct has caused unnecessary costs to the other party.

General points
The reforms were intended to cut the length of trial. Suitable cases may be disposed without a hearing (r.1.4 (2)). The statutory right to jury trial is unaffected in deceit, libel, slander, malicious prosecution and false imprisonment. Generally, hearings must be in open court. There are exceptions where hearings may be in private, such as a case involving a child. Witness statements count as evidence-in-chief. In other words, if you bring a witness, you may not examine her in court if she has already made a statement. Supplementary questions may be asked only for "good reason".

The Woolf Reforms and Alternative Dispute Resolution
Lord Woolf was very keen to promote ADR. Under Rule 1.4 of the **CPR**, the court is under a duty to encourage ADR, where appropriate. The courts have been

very keen to promote ADR, by providing the facilities for it and by penalising parties who refuse to cooperate in ADR. See the chapter on alternatives to the civil courts.

BACKGROUND TO THE "WOOLF REFORMS"

English civil procedure was notoriously adversarial and was often referred to in terms of a battle or game. Until the 1980s, the parties "kept their cards close to the chest" until they were forced to disclose their evidence and arguments, and it was difficult to assess the strength of the opposition's case. This led to a number of problems, which were depicted in the literature of Charles Dickens and identified and discussed in over 60 reports in the twentieth century, prior to Lord Woolf's Report. Some of the major problems identified were:

Delay
This was caused by one or both parties manipulating the pre-trial stages for their own ends. It was in the defendant's interests to delay being ordered to pay damages as long as possible. HC cases took years. The length of trial was dictated by the behaviour of the parties and the case they chose to present, with the court out of control.

Inequality of the parties
A battle is only fair if the parties are of equal strength. In most cases, one party is more powerful, in terms of money, other resources, or information. This is obvious where a consumer is suing a large corporation, or where someone who had suffered negligent surgery is suing a health authority. This inequality allowed the powerful party to dominate the other into submission and, since most cases are settled out of court, it was thought that they often settled on terms more acceptable to the powerful party.

Cost
The cost of litigating in the HC was legendary.

Reforms since the 1980s
The *Civil Justice Review* produced its final report in 1988. Its suggestions attempted to eliminate some of the secretive elements of the pre-trial stage. After its interim report, in 1986, the courts issued Practice Directions to require the exchange of witness statements and make discovery (disclosure) automatic. It even contemplated whether two tiers of civil court were really necessary. Its most radical achievement was the **Courts and Legal Services Act 1990**, which gave the county court the same jurisdiction as the HC, except for certain

procedures such as judicial review. The Act enabled the Lord Chancellor to make rules redistributing civil business, shifting most of it down to the county court, where fees were cheaper and procedure simpler.

Very soon, a committee of the two sides of the legal profession produced another report, *Civil Justice on Trial-The Case for Change* (1993), otherwise known as the Heilbron-Hodge Report. It recommended the pre-trial exchange of skeleton arguments, case management and timetabling by the judge, the reduction of oral argument and an emphasis on shifting civil litigation out of court and into ADR. All of these were introduced by Practice Directions from 1994 onwards, so the seeds of the Woolf recommendations had been sown.

Access to Justice, "The Woolf Report" 1996

Defects identified by Lord Woolf included costs, which often exceeded the claim, power inequality between litigants, uncertainty, incomprehensibility, fragmentation, with no-one responsible overall for civil justice, and over-adversarialism, with parties running the cases and ignoring court rules. He recommended case management, with the courts determining and enforcing realistic timetables and suitable procedures. Defended cases should be allocated to one of three tracks.

The second stage of his inquiry concentrated on medical negligence, housing cases and multi-party actions, where he felt the system failed most conspicuously to meet the needs of litigants. He wanted to improve access to justice for small businesses. He drafted a new set of unified rules for the HC and county court which ultimately became the draft of the **CPR 1998**.

ARE THE WOOLF REFORMS WORKING? EVALUATIVE COMMENTS AND RESEARCH

1. Robert Turner, then Senior Master in the High Court, welcomed the new rules ((2000) 150 N.L.J. 49). The adversarial approach had been replaced by more of co-operation. Settlements were achieved earlier, procedures were defining the real issues between the parties, and solicitors would find the quicker disposal rate allowed them to do more work. In the short term, however, the new rules had not succeeded in attacking cost, because the system was costly at the commencement of the action ("front loaded").

2. A survey of heads of legal departments of UK companies by the law firm Eversheds, found 54 per cent of respondents considered civil litigation improved in 1999–2000. 52 per cent found it quicker but only 22 per cent considered it cheaper. 43 per cent were settling cases earlier. Clients no longer sought aggressive, uncompromising lawyers. Disputes were

handled differently and 41 per cent had used ADR. Only 24 per cent thought litigants were getting better justice. 44 per cent said they were not. 19 per cent said costs had risen.

3. The Civil Justice Council published its first report in September 1999. It was concerned about delay in introducing new IT into the courts.

4. A 2001 Law Society survey of 130 solicitors by the Law Society showed they were concerned that costs assessments were arbitrary and unpredictable, often causing them to make a loss over litigation. New procedures, frontloading work and, consequently, cost, were not cheaper for clients and led to more work. Most considered the use of joint experts inappropriate in multi-track cases.

5. In 2002, the Lord Chancellor's Department published an updated evaluation of the Woolf reforms, confirming their "broad success". The use of pre-action protocols and offers to settle had diverted cases from litigation. Time from issue to trial had dropped from 639 days in 1997, to 498 in 2000–01. There had been a levelling off in the use of ADR: *Civil Justice Reform Evaluation—Further Findings*.

6. A 2002 Court Service survey of court users showed 20 per cent of lawyers found court procedures difficult to understand but 45 per cent of professionals thought the Woolf reforms had simplified procedures.

7. A 2002 joint Law Society/Civil Justice Council report by Goriely and others examined the impact of the Woolf reforms on pre-action behaviour. 54 lawyers, insurers and claims managers were interviewed and 150 pre- and post-Woolf case files were inspected. The research concluded that the Woolf reforms had enhanced access to justice. Early disclosure had led to more settlements at the pre-action stage and they were based on better information. Most practitioners regarded the reforms as a success, citing clearer structure and greater certainty in the fast track. Expert evidence continued to be problematic, although the instruction of agreed experts had almost eradicated the concept of an expert owned by one side. Many felt that the courts were inefficient in listing, because they were under-resourced. Problems caused by lack of IT were well known.

8. For an excellent, well-researched and comprehensive evaluation of "The Woolf reforms in retrospect", see S. Burn in *Legal Action*, July 2003.

9. By 2009, there was widespread concern about disproportionate costs. *Multiplex Constructions UK Ltd. v Cleveland Bridge UK Ltd* [2008] EWHC 2220 (TCC), involved a dispute about the construction of Wembley Stadium. The four year dispute absorbed £22 MILLION in legal costs, including £1 million on photocopying. Multiplex claimed £25 million in damages but Jackson J. ordered only £6.1 million, observing that each party had thrown away golden opportunities to settle. He is now Jackson L.J. and in 2009–10 is conducting a fundamental review of costs.

In his interim report, he points out that fixed costs for fast track cases, as Woolf recommended, were only partly implemented. He is considering contingency and conditional fees, as operated in other jurisdictions, and may repeat the old suggestion of a contingency legal aid fund, contributed to by extracting a portion of all damages recovered, as this is one of the few countries where a claimant can keep all he recovers. See summary by M. Zander at (2009) 159 N.L.J. 743 and A. Wadey at (2009) 159 N.L.J. 706.

10. The Law Society opposed his suggestion of increasing the small claims limit, because thousands of litigants would lose their costs or have to represent themselves, burdening the courts. John McQuater, President of the Association of Personal Injury Lawyers, said the small claims limit for personal injuries should stay at £1,000 because fixed costs were inappropriate for personal injuries. They advantaged well-resourced defendants: (2009) 159 N.L.J. 1079. In a very informative article, however, P. Thomson Q.C. says the small claims limit in PI will have to rise: (2009) 159 N.L.J. 1049. He reminds us that when legal aid was abolished for PI, conditional fees were permitted to fill the gap (see chapter on legal services). Because of our tradition of loser pays on costs, losing defendants had to pay the claimant's CFA success fee and "after the event insurance", creating disproportionate costs bills. Jackson L.J.'s interim report concentrates on remedies through the courts, not alternatives that have grown up, where the party does not need a lawyer. 85 per cent of small claims litigants like the rules as they are, with the parties paying their own costs, according to the Consumers Association, so small claims procedure is doing well without lawyers. Jackson recommends fixed costs in the fast track. Raising the PI small claims limit would upset lawyers but would increase access to justice.

11. Because 2009 was the tenth anniversary of the reforms, there were many evaluative articles. The *New Law Journal* published a series, including one by P. Thompson Q.C., general editor of *The Civil Court Practice*, (2009) 159 N.L.J. 293. He said introducing Money Claims Online in 2002 was a real breakthrough for litigants in person and had "done wonders for access to justice" BUT . . . the fast and multi-tracks "are full of snags and pitfalls for which the litigant in person cannot prepare". The 391 pages of *The County Court Practice* are replaced with 2,301 pages of *The Civil Court Practice*, "a 550% increase!" While there is a QBD guide and a chancery guide there is no *County Courts Guide*. "The aims of simplification and unification of procedures were admirable but they have not been achieved". He suggests making the small claims track the normal track where both sides are LIPs, regardless of the claim and amount. He also suggests that lay representation is the norm in employment tribunals and should be permitted in the courtroom.

12. M. Zander said it was predictable that early preparation of cases had increased costs: (2009) 159 N.L.J. 367. D. Regan complains of judges' failure to tackle the high fees charged by experts and barristers: (2009) 159 N.L.J. 875. Lord Woolf complains of the lack of the IT systems he envisaged and the increase in court costs that far outstrips inflation, *The Times*, June 11, 2009, and says "I was relying on the client controlling the costs . . . The desire to win at all costs has meant that there is still no proper control".

13. DJ David Oldham said electronic filing and document management had been abandoned, except for the Commercial Court. Meanwhile, solicitors swamp courts with email, fax and hard copies of all documents (2009) 159 N.L.J. 1223.

14. For latest research and reports see the Civil Justice Council website. Remember it is their job to monitor the success of the Woolf reforms.

....

CIVIL APPEALS

Appeals from magistrates' courts
As in criminal cases, appeal lies to the Crown Court and takes the form of a full rehearing. In family matters, appeal used to lie to the HC "by way of case stated". This has now been replaced, in 2009, with an appeal to the county court, on the grounds that the decision is wrong in law or in excess of jurisdiction.

Appeals from the county court and High Court from 2000
The Government explained the rationale behind this regime in its 1998 White Paper, *Modernising Justice*. The resulting procedure is contained in the **Access to Justice Act 1999**, in the **CPR 1998**, the amended **Rules of the Supreme Court** and in various Practice Directions. The whole regime is explained by the CA (Civil Division) in *Tanfern Ltd v Cameron-MacDonald* [2000] 1 W.L.R. 1311. The Government planned to achieve its objectives of *proportionality* and *efficiency* by "diverting from the Court of Appeal those cases which, by their nature, do not require the attention of the most senior judges in the country". The principles are as follows:

- Permission to appeal will only be given where the court considers that an appeal would have a *real prospect of success*.
- In normal circumstances, more than one appeal cannot be justified.
- There should be no automatic right to appeal. Leave (now called permission) would be required in virtually all appeals to the CA. (My emphasis).

Jurisdiction

- In fast-track cases heard by a DJ, appeal lies to a circuit judge.
- In those heard by a circuit judge, appeal lies to a HC judge.
- In multi-track cases, all appeals against final orders lie to the CA.
- Appeals against a procedural decision of a DJ will be to a circuit judge; appeals against decisions by a master or circuit judge lie to a HC judge; and those against procedural decisions of a HC judge lie to the CA.
- Exceptional cases involving important points of principle or which affect a number of litigants may go straight to the CA (Civil Division).

Composition

Changes to the composition, procedures, working methods and management of the CA were designed to help it operate more efficiently. Under the **Access to Justice Act 1999,** the CA can now consist of any number of judges, according to the importance and complexity of the case. There should be more emphasis on case management and a more coherent IT infrastructure.

Approach

Generally, every appeal is limited to a review of the decision of the lower court, unless a Practice Direction provides otherwise, or the court considers that it would be in the interests of justice to hold a rehearing.

Grounds

The appeal court will only allow an appeal where the lower court was wrong (in substance) or where it was unjust because of a serious procedural or other irregularity. Now, the decision of the lower court attracts a much greater significance.

Recording decisions

This makes it all the more important for decisions to be recorded accurately.

Powers

Generally, an appeal court has all the powers of the lower court. It also has the power to affirm, set aside or vary any order or judgment of the lower court, to refer any claim or issue for determination by the lower court, to order a new trial or hearing and to make a costs order. In 2000, small claims appeals were placed on the same footing as other civil appeals. The appellant must obtain permission. The appeal is an oral review, not a rehearing.

Second appeals

The CA in *Tanfern* said Parliament had made it clear in the **Access to Justice Act 1999** that second appeals would now be a rarity. The decision of the first appeal court should be given primacy, unless the CA itself considered that the appeal would raise an important point of principle or practice or that there was some other compelling reason for it to hear a second appeal.

Appeals from the Court of Appeal to the UK Supreme Court

An appeal lies from any judgment of the CA. An application for leave must be made first to the CA and, if refused, may be made to the UKSC. Appeals are normally heard by five UKSC justices. The parties must each lodge a printed "case", supposedly being a succinct statement of the arguments below and of the issues before the Court. Theoretically, all justices will have read this "case" and the judgments in the court below in advance of the hearing. This emphasis on written argument has been used to reduce oral argument before the Court. Judgment is normally reserved and the justices' opinions delivered some days or weeks later.

....

FURTHER READING ON CIVIL PROCEDURE

Civil Procedure Rules and Practice Directions, Ministry of Justice website. Also quarterly civil justice statistics on the MoJ website
Darbyshire on the ELS (2008), Chapter 10, material referred to therein and website updates.
Civil Justice Council website.
Civil Justice Quarterly
Most articles and books by Dame Hazel Genn, especially her Hamlyn lectures 2008, *Judging Civil Justice* (Cambridge, 2009), summarised by M. Zander at (2009) 159 N.L.J. 91.

....

REFERENCES TO THE EUROPEAN COURT OF JUSTICE (IN CIVIL AND CRIMINAL CASES)

Queries on the interpretation of a point of Community law can be sent up to the European Court of Justice (ECJ) from a civil or criminal case at any point in the procedure. Article 234 of the EC Treaty (EC) concerns references to the ECJ by domestic courts of Member States:

"(1)   The Court of Justice shall have jurisdiction to give preliminary rulings concerning:

(a)   the interpretation of the Treaty;

(b)   the validity and interpretation of acts of the institutions of the Community and of the ECB;

(c)   the interpretation of the statutes of bodies established by an Act of the Council, where those statutes so provide.

(2)   Where such a question is raised before any court or tribunal of a Member State, that court or tribunal may, if it considers that a decision on the question is necessary to enable it to give judgment, request the Court of Justice to give a ruling thereon.

(3)   Where any such question is raised in a case pending before a court or tribunal of a Member State, against whose decisions there is no judicial remedy under national law, that court or tribunal shall bring the matter before the Court of Justice".

Points to note about Article 234:

1.   Any judicial or quasi-judicial body may refer, however lowly. For instance, magistrates' courts and tribunals.

2.   The "question" may be raised by the parties or the court but only the court may make the reference.

3.   The ruling is preliminary only in the sense that the case then goes back to the original court for it to apply the law to the facts. Obviously, the ECJ's rulings on Community law, etc. are final.

4.   The ECJ will not answer hypothetical questions.

5.   Facts should normally be found before reference but there may be exceptional cases.

6.   The ECJ has accepted the doctrine of *acte clair*. This means that a point need not be referred if it is "reasonably clear and free from doubt".

7.   References under art.234 are discretionary, except where there is no judicial remedy against the domestic court's decision. In that instance, an obligation to refer arises under art. 234(3).

8.   The case in the English or Welsh court is suspended, while the procedure is completed but it takes an average of two years for the ECJ to answer the question sent over, thus causing immense delay.

FURTHER READING ON THE ART. 234 PROCEDURE

Darbyshire on the ELS (2008), Chapter 3, material referred to therein and website updates.
European Court of Justice website.

You should now know and understand:

- why common law procedure is called adversarial;

- how civil cases are distributed between courts;

- civil procedure under the CPR 1998, in outline, including the overriding objective and the importance of pre-action protocols;

- the background to these Woolf reforms: the reasons for them and reforms that preceded them;

- research and commentary evaluating their success, measured against Lord Woolf's intentions;

- basic civil appeal procedure; and

- the art.234 procedure for referring questions of European Community (EU) law to the European Court of Justice, including the notes above.

QUESTION AND ANSWER

The Question

Explain and critically evaluate "the Woolf reforms" to civil procedure.

Advice and the Answer

Advice

"Explain" here means describe the main points, in outline, and explore the reasons why the Woolf reforms were executed. "Critically evaluate", does not mean you have to say something critical about the reforms. Criticism in this context means the same as theatre criticism, which also includes praise and neutral assessment.

Answer guide

1. Explain what is meant by "the Woolf reforms", outlining the main points of the new civil procedure regime (single set of rules in plain English, etc.) and remembering to mention case management, the

overriding objective of the **CPR 1998** and what it means in practice.

2. Explain why civil procedure was reformed, by briefly outlining the main problems identified by Lord Woolf in *Access to Justice*, 1996.

3. Examine critiques of the Woolf reforms outlined in this chapter, ELS textbooks, the Civil Justice Council website and journals such as the *Civil Justice Quarterly*, *Legal Action*, *New Law Journal* and so on. Pay attention to critiques published in journals and newspapers in 2009, as that was the tenth anniversary of the **CPR**. Look out for Jackson L.J.'s final report on costs in 2010, because that is a highly relevant assessment of how the **Rules** are working. Look out also for responses to that report.

4. Beware of straying onto the subject of legal services, which Lord Woolf also considered in *Access to Justice*.

Figure 2

TRIBUNAL STRUCTURE 2010

UK UPPER TRIBUNAL

Senior President (LJ) and Deputy (HC judge)

Immigration & Asylum Chamber	Lands Chamber	Administrative Appeals Chamber	Tax & Chancery Chamber
Immigration and asylum appeals	Jurisdiction formerly exercised by the Lands Tribunal (land appeals)	Appeals from the chambers below, on points of law; judicial review of criminal injuries comp; appeals from Traffic Commissioners; appeals from the General Regulatory Chamber.	Appeals from Tax & Duties Chamber; charity appeals; pension regulation; financial services.
President, Vice President, (HC judges), other HC judges, circuit judges, UT immigration judges	President, Vice President, (HC judges), other HC judges, circuit judges, UT judges	President, VP, HC judges, circuit judges, UT judges	President, VP, HC and circuit chancery judges, Upper Tribunal judges, non-legal members

Appeals on point of law or judicial review →

FIRST TIER TRIBUNAL

Immigration & Asylum Chamber	War Pensions & Armed Forces Compensation Chamber	Social Entitlement Chamber	Health, Education & Social Care Chamber	General Regulatory Chamber	Tax & Duties Chamber
Immigration and asylum	War pensions and armed forces compensation	Asylum support; social security and child support; criminal injuries compensation; housing benefit; council tax benefit, etc.	Care standards; mental health review; special educational needs and disability; family health services appeals.	Charities; consumer credit appeals; estate agents; transport; gambling; claims management services; information appeals; immigration services.	Tax, VAT and duties.
President, Deputies (circuit judges), First Tier immigration judges, non-legal members	President, Deputies (circuit judges),First Tier tribunal judges, members of armed forces	President, Deputies, First Tier tribunal judges	President, Deputies, lay members, doctors, psychiatrists, etc.	President, etc.	President, non-legal members, etc.

Employment Appeal Tribunal

Employment Appeals

President (High Court judge), HC and circuit judges, employment judges, non-legal members

Employment Tribunals

Unfair dismissal; redundancy; discrimination, etc.

Employment judges and non-legal members

Employment is not part of the new structure.

Most first instance appeals will be heard in the First Tier Tribunal. The Upper Tribunal is a Superior Court of Record, like the High Court. Appeals from the UT on important points of law lie to the Court of Appeal. Non-legal members sit in some UT and some FTT cases (in accordance with the tribunals they replaced). The relationship with the High Court over judicial review is 'under development' in December 2009. Court of Appeal judges may sit in the UT.

Alternatives to the Civil Courts

5

INTRODUCTION

In the nineteenth and twentieth centuries, some alternative forums to the civil courts were established.

- Tribunals: Parliament has allocated some disputes to them by statute, mainly appeals against state decisions.
- Arbitration: private dispute resolution, invented in the industrial revolution, for the speedy resolution of disputes. Awards are legally binding and arbitration is regulated by the Arbitration Act 1996.
- ADR (alternative dispute resolution): all the other types of private dispute resolution, developed since the 1970s, mainly informal but some are statutory.

> **KEY POINT**
>
> While the litigant may choose to take a dispute to arbitration or use ADR, they **cannot *choose* to go to a tribunal**. Parliament made the choice in the many Acts of Parliament creating tribunals.

TRIBUNALS

What are tribunals and how do they compare with courts?

Until 2009, tribunals were too disparate to be described as a "system", though the main ones are being restructured, following the Tribunals, Courts and Enforcement Act 2007. There were over 100 sets of tribunals, each highly specialised, dealing with only one area of the law. Most deal with disputes between the citizen and the state, for instance, over tax, state benefits, school allocation and so on. Others adjudicate between private parties, such as employment tribunals. Some tribunals form a nationwide network, such as the new Social Entitlement Chamber, whilst others are one central unit.

Why did over 100 sets of tribunals develop alongside, but outside, the court system?

Most were created in the twentieth century. As the welfare state grew, they were developed to adjudicate between citizen and state because the Labour and Liberal Governments which developed state power distrusted the (Conservative) judiciary.

The Franks Committee was established to examine concern over this bureaucratisation, and reported, in 1957, that tribunals should be seen as performing a judicial, not an executive, function and they should be better regulated. They identified four main reasons for their popularity:

- cheapness (no formal buildings or judicial regalia, or court fees, etc.);
- accessibility and speed;
- freedom from technicality so people could supposedly represent themselves; and
- expert knowledge (of the panel).

Criticisms
- They were separate and administered separately. This was confusing, inefficient and wasteful.
- Some had become so court-like that the litigant struggled without a lawyer, yet legal aid was not and still is not available before most tribunals. For example, lawyers often represent appellants before the Employment Appeal Tribunal on a voluntary basis, because employment law is very complex. Unrepresented parties cause problems for the tribunal panel. Research demonstrates that representation by anyone enhances the applicant's chances of success.
- Some now have bigger delays than the courts.
- Some are so court-like, with complexity and delay, that they have lost any advantage over the courts and applicants are encouraged to use ADR.
- Lack of visibility.
- They do not follow precedent and are thus unpredictable (though those with an appellate level follow appeal precedents).
- Informality can lead to a lack of due process.
- See further Leggatt below.

The Leggatt Report
A review by Sir Andrew Leggatt was published in 2001: *Tribunals for Users-One System, One Service*. Below are the main points.

- It concentrated on the 70 bodies which provided specialist adjudication which would otherwise be dealt with by the courts.

- It suggested that tribunals should be used, instead of courts, where users could present their own cases; where expertise was a major issue; and where a tribunal could effectively deal with issues of mixed fact and law.
- Problems were: isolation leading to duplication of effort; lack of resources and IT; and delays and poor communication with users.
- Some tribunal members felt they could not be seen as independent of the government departments administering them.
- Leggatt rejected creating a separate system of administrative courts, as exists in European legal systems.
- Independence could only be assured by separating tribunals from government departments and forming them into a coherent system, directed by a board and administered by a Tribunals Service and the Department of Constitutional Affairs ("DCA") (now Ministry of Justice).
- The civil justice reforms should be applied to tribunal procedure.
- Confusing overlaps with court jurisdiction should be removed.
- The tribunals system should be divided by subject-matter into eight subject sections, with a single appellate division in each.
- Judicial review should be excluded. Appeals on law should go to the Court of Appeal.
- Tribunal members should be trained by the Judicial Studies Board, in interpersonal skills.
- A Judicial Appointments Commissioner should supervise appointments.
- Government departments should consider introducing internal review procedures to ensure that their case is correct in fact and law and that opposing the citizen's appeal was a justifiable use of public funds. They should disseminate lessons learned from tribunals.

Government response

They started implementing these recommendations before he reported, such as on appointment and training of tribunal members. In 2002, the Law Commission set out plans for reforming the eight tribunals for resolving land, valuation and housing disputes. This follows the recommendation for a clearer structure for users, without unnecessary overlaps. Also in 2002, the Government announced that it had accepted the 61 reform recommendations of the Employment Tribunal System's Taskforce. In 2006, a new unified Tribunals Service came into operation.

In 2004, Government published a White Paper (a document containing plans for legislation), *Transforming Public Services: Complaints, Redress and Tribunals*. It examined not just tribunals but the whole administrative justice system and dispute resolution process, with the aim of "helping to improve standards of decision making" and providing better redress where things go wrong so that fewer cases come before tribunals. The Government intended to create a Senior President of Tribunals, a Tribunals Rule Committee, a more coherent system of appeals and reviews and a replacement for the supervisory Council on Tribunals. Panel members would be renamed "tribunal judge". The **Tribunals, Courts and Enforcement Act 2007** provides a Senior President (a Lord Justice of Appeal, who was appointed in 2005), heading a "simplified statutory framework" to provide more coherence, organised as in the diagram, from 2009–10. It replaced the Council on Tribunals with an Administrative Justice and Tribunals Council, with a broader remit.

Tribunal Members

Chairmen of tribunals, now usually called tribunal judges, are normally members of the legal profession, sitting as part-timers. Lawyer-chairmen were favoured by the Franks Committee in 1957. As a result of the **Constitutional Reform Act 2005**, from 2006 tribunal judges are appointed by the Lord Chancellor after selection competitions run by the Judicial Appointments Commission.

The two "wingers" who sit with the tribunal judge are usually not legally qualified but are selected for their expertise. For example, employment tribunal and employment appeal tribunal members are usually drawn from employers' and employees' organisations; those tribunals concerned with the collection of revenue often appoint accountants, and so on. In 2009, there were about 8,000 non-lawyers who sat on tribunals. The Government has been criticised for abolishing lay involvement in some tribunals, in the late 1990s, notably social security tribunals. Tribunal training is undertaken by the Judicial Studies Board, as Leggatt recommended.

ARBITRATION

Arbitration is the commercial world's alternative to slow, expensive and incon-venient High Court litigation. It means the adjudication of a dispute, usually by an individual expert in the subject-matter involved, or a lawyer. It is more formal than ADR and results in a legally binding decision. Arbitration is regulated by the **Arbitration Act 1996**. The arbitrator will normally follow the same stages as civil litigation but submissions are often written and hearings may be by tele-phone. Most arbitral rules permit the arbitrator to act inquisitorially, that is, asking questions. She is not bound by strict rules of evidence or substantive law so, if the parties agree, she can decide according to equity and good conscience. She gives a reasoned decision, enforceable in court. An award may be challenged in court for three reasons:

- Jurisdiction;
- a point of law of general public importance; or
- a serious irregularity.

The Act has been subject to a lot of interpretation. In *Warborough Investments Ltd. v S. Robinson & Sons (Holdings) Ltd.* [2003] EWCA Civ 751, the CA held that under s.1, the courts were required to accord to arbitrators a reasonably wide discretion.

Arbitration may arise in one of three ways:

By contract The parties may have entered a contract, in some context such as shipping or insurance, and, in a clause, they have agreed to refer any disputes arising under the contract to an arbitrator (who may be named in the contract). This is significant, not just because it is common trade practice, but also because lay people are often, unwittingly, parties to an arbitration clause. For instance, almost all insurance policies contain an arbitration clause BUT where a business contracts with a consumer, they must fully explain any arbitration clause and an arbitration clause will automatically be deemed unfair where disputes are for less than £5,000, under delegated legislation, confirmed in *Mylcrist Builders v Buck* [2008] EWHC 2172 (TCC).

If one of the parties tries to ignore such a clause and goes to court, the court may order a "stay" (a stop) of proceedings so that the matter may be referred to arbitration BUT In *Allianz SpA and Another v West Tankers Inc* Case C-185/07, 10 Feb 2009, *Times*, 13 Feb, 2009, the ECJ ruled that a court in one EU Member State had no power to rule that a party should drop a case in another EU state on the ground that the parties had agreed to refer any dispute to arbitration. Under Regulation 44/2001, the Member State's court had the exclusive power to rule on its own jurisdiction.

By reference from the court A judge in the Commercial Court may refer a dispute to an arbitrator.

By agreement Once a dispute has arisen, the parties may choose to go to an arbitrator rather than a court, in same way that they may choose ADR, below.

Background

The rise of arbitration occurred in the late nineteenth century when trade associations wished to have their disputes privately, cheaply and speedily resolved by experts, for instance, construction disputes involving Britain's new railway network, or arguments about liability for a ship's rotting cargo. London is an important international arbitration centre, always worried about losing its market-share to other international arbitration centres, such as Paris, Singapore, New York etc. A closely related procedure is "adjudication", used in the construction industry, where an adjudicator is expected to make a swift decision.

Advantages
- speed;
- privacy, important where commercial, sensitive information is involved;
- finality;
- expertise—the arbitrator will be an expert and some are also lawyers;
- low cost (the parties pay privately for the arbitrator);
- the International Convention on the Recognition and Enforcement of Foreign Arbitral Awards obliges contracting states to recognise foreign arbitral awards;
- unlike ADR, the decision is final and binding, the arbitrator is regulated by the 1996 Act and parties can appeal to the courts.

Advantages of London in international arbitrations
- Use of English law: many international contracts stipulate that English law governs the contract.
- London's financial and commercial power.
- Position in international time zones.
- Historically, it is an international maritime and insurance centre and international law firms use it as a springboard into Europe.

Disadvantages
- It has become lawyer-dominated and can be expensive.
- Appeal to the courts is possible in England so this destroys finality.
- We are subject to international criticism that our courts interfere too much. In *Lesotho Highlands Development Authority v Impregilo SpA* [2005] UKHL 43, the HL reminded us that the philosophy of the 1996 Act was to drastically reduce the extent of court intervention.
- Practitioners prefer to arbitrate in Paris, because of our labour-intensive, expensive emphasis on document disclosure, longer hearings, the cultural arrogance of English lawyers, convinced their methods are superior, and the use of barristers and judges as arbitrators, who attempt to replicate court procedure. (See interviews in an article by Smulian, Law Society's *Gazette*, June 19, 2003).

ALTERNATIVE DISPUTE RESOLUTION (ADR)

The phrase was imported from the US in about 1990 but mediation was being developed in England and Wales from the 1970s. Lord Chancellors Mackay and Irvine (1980–2003) took an active interest in ADR, as a means of avoiding the public and private expense and the private pain of litigation. Since the mid-1990s, civil advocates have been required to inform their clients of ADR (It is now a requirement of the **Civil Procedure Rules 1998**, r.1). There are three main categories: mediation, conciliation and arbitration (above). Schemes may be private or court-linked.

Mediation
This is the least formal. The parties voluntarily refer their dispute to an independent third party who will discuss the issues with both sides and, by acting as a "go-between", will assist them to discuss and negotiate areas of conflict and identify and settle certain issues. It will only be successful if parties are willing to compromise. It is not appropriate for disputes where there is little room for compromise such as housing possession proceedings.

Conciliation
This lies midway between informal mediation and formal arbitration. The process is very similar to mediation but the third party may offer a non-binding opinion which may lead to a settlement.

Other types are self-explanatory
They include early neutral evaluation, expert determination, mini-trial by a privately hired judge, expert determination and online dispute resolution
  Note: ADR is not suitable where the parties want a court to clarify the law or where only a court order will do, e.g. an injunction to prevent a threatened breach of the law.

Examples of use of ADR
* The best known mediation schemes are those offered to family disputants. Thousands of people, notably solicitors, were trained as mediators to satisfy the mediation requirements of the **Family Law Act 1996**. Public funding can be obtained for it. Under the Law Society's Family Law Protocol 2002, unless inappropriate, solicitors are required to explain mediation and collaboration to clients. By 2005, over 250 lawyers had been trained in "collaborative law", a no-court, non-adversarial scheme originating in the USA. The government and courts strongly encourage family mediation and in-court conciliation, because of the extremely high

court costs and legal aid costs of protracted family disputes but research reached mixed conclusions on success (L. Trinder and J. Kellett MoJ Research Report 15/07, MoJ website). It is not appropriate where violence has been alleged or where drug/alcohol abuse is involved.

- Welsh NHS trusts piloted mediation in clinical negligence disputes and it was copied in England in the NHS Redress Scheme. Even a multi-million pound damages action for birth injuries cost only about £10,000 to mediate, whereas it might cost £150,000 to litigate in the civil courts.
- The government announced in 2001 that it would be using ADR in its disputes. It saved £6 million in 2002–03.
- The Technology & Construction Court has introduced a court settlement process. Parties may request the help of specially trained judges in reaching an amicable settlement.
- In 2005, the Government launched a national mediation helpline, to put callers in touch with an accredited mediator.
- The Legal Services Commission announced in February 2009 that it would spend £100,000 in supporting trainee mediators.

Will the courts enforce ADR?

- The Commercial Court has always been very keen to divert part or the whole of a case to ADR or arbitration, because they know how slow and costly HC proceedings are. Coleman J. enforced a mediation clause in a commercial contract in *Cable & Wireless PLC v IBM UK Ltd* [2002] EWHC 2059.
- The CA has been equally keen. In the leading case of *Dunnett v Railtrack* [2002] EWCA Civ 303, they held that where a party refused to cooperate in ADR, they might be penalised in costs. They reminded the parties that they had a duty to further the overriding objective of the **Civil Procedure Rules**. (As can be seen from the civil procedure chapter, this includes "saving expense"). As a result of this, statistics published by the Centre for Effective Dispute Resolution (CEDR), showed an increase in ADR.
- The courts backtracked, in *Halsey v Milton Keynes General NHS Trust* [2004] EWCA 576, holding that compulsion would be a breach of art.6 (fair trial) of the **European Convention on Human Rights** because it constrained access to the courts.
- In a May 2008 speech (Judiciary website), the Master of the Rolls acknowledged that *Halsey* might have been over-cautious. Compulsory ADR did not breach art.6 and was indeed referred to in the EC Directive on Mediation. Compulsory mediation had been introduced in a number of US jurisdictions, demonstrating that compulsion did not breach common law or European fair trial rights.

- Many courts have established court-based mediation schemes and renamed themselves Civil Justice Centres. Following an unsuccessful mediation experiment in 1996, the Central London County Court renamed itself and in 2004 started a scheme of automatic referral. Twenty random cases per week, above the small claims limit, are automatically referred to mediation. If parties object, they have to give reasons and a district judge decides whether these are acceptable. If a party still refuses to mediate, for reasons unacceptable to the judge, they risk being liable to pay costs. Manchester County Court renamed itself Manchester Civil Justice Centre and it introduced a mediation adviser. In 2007, the L.C. reported that 86 per cent of mediations in one year settled on the day.
- **Directive 2008/52/EC** encourages the use of mediation in cross-border disputes. It obliges EU Member States to encourage training and gives every judge the right to suggest mediation.

Attitudes to ADR

- Generally, judges were very quick to latch on to ADR and strongly promoted it from about 1990 but lawyers were very slow to accept it. There was very low uptake. In the Central London County Court 1996 scheme only five per cent of parties agreed to ADR, research by Genn demonstrating widespread ignorance by lawyers and fear of showing weakness. In 1998–99, parties in only 12 of 250 CA cases accepted ADR. Take-up of the Commercial Court's ADR scheme was "modest" in 1996–2000 (all researched by Genn).
- A big boost came from r.1 of the **CPR 1998** and a critical core of big law firms started offering it.
- Another breakthrough came when the Law Society and ADR Group successfully challenged in court the refusal of legal aid for non-family ADR.
- The Centre for Effective Dispute Resolution audits the use of ADR and the 2007 audit claimed a 33 per cent growth in the previous two years (for latest audit, see CEDR website).
- The family lawyers' group Resolution said the use of collaborative law in divorce proceedings had increased by 87 per cent in 2006–7.

BUT SOME PARTIES STILL WANT THEIR DAY IN COURT . . .

A neighbour boundary dispute over who owns a worthless 6m square shrub patch has already cost the defendant £70,000 and will proceed to the CA in autumn 2009. Had it been mediated, it would have cost about £5,000–£6000: (2009) 159 N.L.J. 1077.

You should now know and understand:

- why tribunals grew up outside the court system, what issues they deal with, and how they were thought to be better for the litigant;

- the criticisms that were made, prompting the Leggatt Review;

- Leggatt's recommendations and how these translated into the 2007 Act and the structure in the diagram;

- that unlike ADR and arbitration, a party cannot choose to go to a tribunal;

- what arbitration is, why it developed, how it differs from ADR (statutory regulation and enforcement by and appeal to the courts) and its advantages and disadvantages; and

- what is meant by ADR (with examples), why and how the courts and Government are keen to promote it (advantages over litigation) and how it has developed since 1990.

FURTHER READING/UPDATING

Darbyshire on the ELS, 2008, Chapter 11, and materials listed therein.
Civil Justice Quarterly
New Law Journal
Public Law

Websites
Administrative Justice and Tribunals Council (including comprehensive summary of academic and research papers)
CEDR (on ADR)
Chartered Institute of Arbitrators
Judiciary (judges' speeches)
Leggatt Review
Ministry of Justice
Tribunals Service

QUESTION AND ANSWER

The Question

Give an account of the development of ADR in England and Wales and explore the reasons for its rise in popularity.

Advice and the answer

Advice
Do not get distracted into describing types of ADR at any length. This is such simple information that it does not demonstrate intelligence or analytical skill or real understanding.

Answer guide
1. *Briefly* explain what is meant by ADR and give examples. Your textbook will provide this information. There is no need to resort to dictionary definitions or Wikipedia.
2. "Give an account of" means tell the story of. This story is explained at greater length in *Darbyshire on the ELS* (2008).
3. Explain the advantages of ADR, especially cheapness, speed and informality.
4. Explain how ADR was generally imported from the US and was promoted by Lord Chancellors Irvine and Mackay in their policies and speeches.
5. Explain how it has been emphasised in the **Civil Procedure Rules 1998**, since 1999 and promoted by the Government in its litigation.
6. Explain how it has been promoted through court-annexed schemes and how the CA have promoted it by penalising litigants who have persisted in civil litigation rather than considering ADR (*Dunnett v Railtrack*, etc.).
7. Explain how it has been promoted by making public funding (legal aid) available for use in ADR such as mediation.
8. Mention that research demonstrated lawyers' initial reluctance to use ADR.
9. Read and cite articles and statistics from the CEDR website, which is one of the best sources of material evaluating the popularity of ADR at your time of writing and over the previous years.
10. Check the Civil Justice Council website for research on ADR and annual reports.
11. In your conclusion, briefly outline what you have just said.

Criminal Procedure

6

INTRODUCTION

In common law systems, criminal procedure, like civil procedure, is adversarial, with prosecution and defence responsible for adducing evidence and bringing legal argument to establish their case. (The European Convention on HR also requires that criminal proceedings are adversarial). The court is not involved in directing investigations. While civil procedure is straightforward, criminal procedure is much more complex. It has been bedevilled by constant changes in recent years, as each Home Secretary tries to demonstrate how "tough on crime" he is, promoting layer upon layer of criminal justice legislation, which is very difficult for the courts to apply and lawyers to understand, let alone the public. In this chapter we will examine the following.

- The fundamental rules of criminal procedure, deriving from the common law, the **European Convention on Human Rights 1950** and the Criminal Procedure Rules 2005.
- Pre-trial criminal procedure.
- The trial process, both criminal and civil.
- The appeal process.
- The post-appeal process for re-examining alleged miscarriages of justice.

BACKGROUND: REFORM BODIES

In 1990–91, faith in the criminal process plummeted, with the acknowledgment by the Court of Appeal (Criminal Division) (CACD) of a number of miscarriages of justice which had resulted in many innocent people spending decades in gaol. The most notable were the Guildford Four, the Maguires, and the Birmingham Six. In 1991, the Home Secretary appointed a Royal Commission on Criminal Justice (RCCJ), which reported in 1993. Its terms of reference were to examine the effectiveness of the criminal process in securing the conviction of the guilty and the acquittal of the innocent. Its recommendations were heavily criticised, since many bolstered the power of prosecutors. In 1997, the Home Secretary received a *Review of Delay in the Criminal Justice System*, better known as the Narey Report. Many of Narey's recommendations were enacted in the Crime and Disorder Act 1998. In 2000, the Lord Chancellor asked Lord Justice Auld to conduct yet another review of the criminal process, published in 2001 as the *Review of the Criminal Courts of England and Wales* but known as the Criminal Courts Review. The Bar Council, Liberty, the Law Society and others published responses and the Government responded in a 2002 white paper (a document outlining legislative plans), *Justice for All*. Many of Auld L.J.'s recommendations were accepted and enacted in the **Courts Act 2003** and the Criminal Justice Act 2003.

....

LEGAL FRAMEWORK

Common Law Safeguards for the Accused

KEY POINT

Remembering that our legal system is very old and the mother of all common law legal systems worldwide, there are some fundamental safeguards which our courts apply and which we exported to our common law daughters and which formed the model for the **European Convention on Human Rights 1950**.

* The *"rule of law"* means that the authorities must demonstrate a legal basis for the exercise of power.
* The *presumption of innocence* means that the *burden of proof* is always on the prosecutor to prove guilt (although the accused has some burdens in an increasing number of crimes and this has been heavily criticised).
* The *right of silence* is not ancient but had come to be seen as a right by the end of the twentieth century.
* The right is part of the common law *privilege against self-incrimination*.
* The *quantum (degree) of proof* in common law systems is very high: *proof beyond reasonable doubt*. Thus, it is much more difficult to prove a criminal case than a civil one, where, the degree of proof is merely "on the balance of probabilities".
* The *requirement for a fair trial* was developed by common law judges in the *rules of natural justice*: the accused has a right to know the case against them and the trial tribunal must not be biased or have an interest in the proceedings.
* Furthermore, given the might of the state against the individual accused, there are certain *protective rules*, such as those restricting prosecution evidence, designed to compensate for that inherent imbalance.

- An accused in detention may apply for a writ of *habeas corpus*, asking the court to declare his detention to be unlawful, under the Habeas Corpus Act 1679. This is based on an ancient Anglo-Saxon common law writ, older than Magna Carta 1215.
- The right to *speedy trial* and the 500 year old *rule against torture* (explored in *A and Others v SS for the Home Dept (No 2)* [2005] UKHL 71) are ancient common law rules, providing the basis of art.3 and art.5 (below) respectively.

The European Convention on Human Rights 1950

KEY POINT

British lawyers drafted the European Convention on Human Rights 1950 in the aftermath of World War II and thus incorporated these common law safeguards into the Convention. It was made enforceable in our courts since 2000, as a consequence of the Human Rights Act 1998. Articles 3, 5 and 6 are most pertinent to criminal procedure. Article 6 provides for a right to a fair trial and art.5 a right to liberty and security.

Article 6
- entitles the accused to a fair and public hearing
- within a reasonable time
- by an independent and impartial tribunal established by law.
- He is presumed innocent and
- has the right to be informed, in detail, of the case against him.
- He must have adequate time and facilities to prepare his defence.
- He may defend himself in person,
- or have a choice of free legal assistance if the interests of justice so require.
- He has the right to examine witnesses and
- to have an interpreter if he cannot understand the language of the court.

Article 5
- prescribes the circumstances in which a person may be arrested and detained.
- He must be informed why he has been arrested and what he is charged with.
- He must be brought before a judge within a reasonable time or released.
- All detained persons have a right to challenge the lawfulness of their detention.

Article 3 prohibits torture and inhumane and degrading treatment.

The Criminal Procedure Rules 2005

KEY POINT

For centuries, there have been calls for criminal procedure rules and the criminal law to be codified, as they are throughout Europe and in many common law countries such as the US. Unfortunately, the latest attempt, in the 21st century, has stalled.

Auld L.J. reiterated this in his *Review*. A new Criminal Procedure Rule Committee was created in 2004, as a result of his recommendation, and this devised the first ever set of **Criminal Procedure Rules** in 2005, as a step towards codification. Also, instead of practice rules (guidelines not law) being set out in a mish-mash of Directions, there is now one Consolidated Criminal Practice Direction. The **Criminal Justice Act 2003** prescribes that the Committee must aim, through the Rules, to make the criminal justice system *"accessible fair and efficient"* and the Rules must be simple and be simply expressed. The Rules contain an *"overriding objective"* and rules of case management, reminiscent of the **Civil Procedure Rules 1998**, described in the last chapter. The Lord Chief Justice and Lord Chancellor sought to bring about a "culture change" in the criminal courts, with judges and case managers taking control over case progression. They were concerned about the number of trials that were delayed or ineffective because of lack of preparedness of the lawyers or other agencies, or because of lawyers' delaying tactics. **Rule 1.1** prescribes "the overriding objective of this new code is that criminal cases be dealt with justly". This includes

- acquitting the innocent and convicting the guilty;
- dealing with prosecution and defence fairly;
- recognising the defendant's rights;
- respecting the interests of witnesses, victims and jurors; and
- dealing with cases efficiently and speedily.

The case should be dealt with in ways that take into account the gravity of the offence, the complexity of the issues, the severity of the consequences and the needs of other cases. Part 3 places the criminal courts under a *duty to manage* cases actively, which is novel in the English legal system. This includes

- early identification of issues and the needs of witnesses;
- timetabling and monitoring case progress;
- ensuring evidence is presented in the shortest and clearest way;

CRIMINAL PROCEDURE

- discouraging delay and unnecessary hearings;
- encouraging co-operation; and
- making use of IT.

Case progression officers monitor progress pre-trial, by keeping in touch with all parties: prosecution, defence, etc. A judge, magistrate or clerk may manage a case. The court may set out the consequences of failing to comply with directions. This includes penalising defence lawyers or others. An Effective Trial Management Programme was piloted from 2003. The new Office of Criminal Justice Reform reported in 2008 that ineffective trials had been reduced from 23 per cent in 2002 to 12 per cent in 2007. Rules were passed in 2004 to penalise in costs any third party who causes a case to collapse, such as a newspaper publishing a prejudicial pre-trial report, or someone intimidating witnesses.

THE PRE-TRIAL CRIMINAL PROCESS

Prosecutors
The Attorney General (AG)

She is a government minister and their chief legal adviser, responsible for the Treasury Solicitor's Department, CPS, Revenue and Customs Prosecution Office and Serious Fraud Office. In 2009, she published a Protocol setting out her relationship with them (on her website). She heads the Law Officers' Department and is in overall charge of the prosecution process. Her consent is required by statute for prosecutions of national interest or sensitivity (e.g. certain prosecutions under the Official Secrets Act). She can also enter a *nolle prosequi*, to stop a prosecution (e.g. if it is vexatious or he discovers the defendant is dying).

The Director of Public Prosecutions (DPP)

In addition to heading the CPS and the Serious Organised Crime Agency, dozens of statutes require his consent to prosecution, mostly to serious offences, but he is very seldom involved personally in a decision. In 1997, the Law Commission suggested drastic reduction in the number of offences where the AG's or DPP's consent is required and Auld L.J. agreed, in his 2001 Review. The HL held, in *Kebilene* [2000] 2 A.C. 326 that the DPP's decision to prosecute is not judicially reviewable in the absence of bad faith or dishonesty. In *R (on the application of Purdy) v DPP* [2009] UKHL 45 the law lords ruled that the DPP was obliged to publish his policy identifying the facts and circumstances he would take into account in deciding whether to prosecute someone for assisting the suicide of a terminally ill person.

Public bodies

Many government departments and agencies have statutory prosecution powers.

Private persons

Private prosecutions were preserved on the recommendation of the Royal Commission on Criminal Procedure (RCCP)1981.

The Crown Prosecution Service (CPS)

This was created as a national prosecution service by the Prosecution of Offences Act 1985, on the recommendation of the RCCP. Until then, most prosecutions were instituted by the police, from individual constabularies. This was thought undesirable as they lacked independence. The creation of the CPS allowed for a co-ordinated national prosecution policy. The CPS has the discretion to prosecute and stop proceedings. It can ask the police to investigate offences but it cannot order them to do so. It has no investigatory facilities. The RCCJ 1993 considered whether the CPS should have the power to supervise police investigations, as in Scotland or European jurisdictions. It decided against it but recommended strengthening police consultation with the CPS.

The Narey Report 1997 recommended that CPS non-lawyers should be able to prosecute guilty pleas in the magistrates' court and this was permitted by the **Crime and Disorder Act 1998**. This has been extended to summary trials (following "not guilty" pleas) and contested bail applications, by the Criminal Justice and Immigration Act 2008. This is a money-saving exercise, heavily condemned by the Law Society and the Bar Council, and an internal CPS survey found that only half their 400 paralegals felt they had enough training for this. The Narey Report recommended putting CPS staff into police stations to create a closer working relationship. This was done, despite the criticism that it jeopardises the independence of the CPS.

Prosecution Procedure: Charging and Prosecuting

The Criminal Justice Act 2003, Sch.2 provides that the custody police officer must refer to guidance from the DPP. This indicates which cases should be referred to the CPS and lists those defendants who should be bailed. The Act (s.29) introduces a new way of initiating criminal proceedings. A written charge may be issued by the police or a prosecutor, with a requisition to appear in court. This follows recommendations by Auld L.J. in his *Review* (Ch.10). Allowing prosecutors to issue charges was introduced because they, being lawyers, were more likely to select the appropriate charges than police officers. This was introduced in 2004, after pilot schemes resulted in a 40 per cent increase in early guilty pleas and a 90 per cent decrease in discontinued, ineffective or changed cases. The CPS is guided in its decisions whether to prosecute by the *Code for Crown Prosecutors*. It applies a two-stage test on *evidential sufficiency* and *public interest*. There is no obligation to prosecute all crimes, in contrast with some European jurisdictions. A decision not to prosecute is not normally judicially reviewable. It is not a prosecutor's duty to obtain a conviction at all costs but to act as a minister of justice: *Randall v R.* [2002] UKPC 19.

Cautions

Police detainees may be released with no further action or officially cautioned, including conditionally cautioned, if they admit an offence. Most young offenders are cautioned. The **2003 Act** permits the CPS to issue a conditional caution, where there is sufficient evidence to charge a suspect with an offence which he or she admits, and the suspect agrees. If the suspect fails to comply with the conditions, he may be prosecuted for the offence. The formal caution was recommended by Auld L.J., to replace the informal and piecemeal schemes which were developed by the police over the twentieth century. Cautioning for young offenders was put on a statutory footing in the **Crime and Disorder Act 1998**.

Bail

Most people are tried in magistrates' courts and are not remanded at all, in custody or on bail. The police may grant bail at the police station and the **Criminal Justice Act 2003** enables "street bail" from the scene of the arrest (s.4). The Bail Act 1976 introduced a statutory right to bail. Magistrates may refuse bail only if they believe the defendant will fail to surrender to custody, or commit an offence or will interfere with witnesses. The court must have regard to the nature and seriousness of the offence and the probable disposal of the defendant, his character and community ties, etc. his previous bail record and the strength of evidence against him.

During the late 1980s, concern arose over the number of offences committed whilst on bail. The Criminal Justice and Public Order Act 1994 added another exception to the right to bail, where the defendant was already on bail at the time of the alleged new offence. This has been amended in the **Criminal Justice Act 2003**. There is now a *presumption* that bail will not be granted in these circumstances to an adult unless the court is satisfied that there is no significant risk of his re-offending on bail (s.13). There is also a *presumption* that an adult who has failed to surrender to custody will not be granted bail, unless the court is satisfied that there is no significant risk that he would so fail if released (s.15). There is also a *presumption* against bail for certain Class A drug users (s.19). The **1994 Act** prohibited bail for those charged with murder, rape, manslaughter and attempts of those crimes, where they have previously been convicted of such an offence. Because of the European Convention on HR, this had to be amended by the **Crime and Disorder Act 1998**, to permit the court to grant bail in exceptional circumstances, because under the Convention, a state cannot make a blanket ban on bail for a group of offenders. Bail may be granted by the police, or magistrates' court, or Crown Court. A magistrates' clerk (legal adviser) may renew bail and any court must consider bail at each court appearance. Both prosecution and defence may appeal a bail decision.

The right of silence and the privilege against self-incrimination

The right is a common law right (not ancient) and is closely related to the privilege, again a common law concept, now recognised as part of art.6 of the Convention. The right of silence exists at three stages: on the street, under interrogation and at trial. Until the **Criminal Justice and Public Order Act 1994**, the defendant had an unfettered right to silence and the judge could comment to the jury if a defendant remained silent but could not comment adversely. The right was considered by the Criminal Law Revision Committee 1972, the RCCP 1981 and the RCCJ 1993 and it has long been a subject of controversy.

Proponents   hail it as a major (almost symbolic) safeguard of the English legal system that the defendant cannot convict himself out of his own mouth. It leaves the burden of proof entirely on the prosecution.

Opponents   say it is a rule protecting the guilty; it encourages the police to intimidate suspects into confessing and it is sentimental to argue that the accused should not be allowed to convict himself.

From 1987, Conservative Home Secretaries contemplated limiting the right, because they thought professional criminals took advantage of it. Prior to 1994, one major inroad, which provoked criticism, was the power of the Serious Fraud Office (SFO) to require answers to written questions. In *Saunders v UK* (1997) 23 E.H.R.R. 313 the European Court of Human Rights (ECtHR) ruled that powers exercised by the Department of Trade and Industry, under the Companies Act 1985, to require a defendant to answer questions put to him pre-trial, offended against the privilege against self-incrimination so the offending legislation and other similar Acts were amended by the UK Parliament to prevent answers gained being used in evidence. The Court has ruled that the requirement that the defendant submit to blood and urine tests does not breach the privilege. They also ruled that there is no violation of the privilege by asking car owners to disclose driver details when caught on a speed camera: *Francis v UK* (25624/02) (2008) 46 E.H.R.R. 21.

The RCCJ 1993 recommended that the right of silence under interrogation should be retained and that only after the prosecution case had been fully disclosed should the defendant be required to answer charges, or risk an adverse comment at trial on any new, undisclosed defence (an "ambush defence"). The **1994 Act** went much further than this and, critics said, abrogated the right to silence. Sections 34–39 allow the court to draw "such inferences as appear proper" from the accused's failure to mention, under police questioning, any fact which he could have been expected to mention, or failure (under questioning) to account for any objects, marks or substances, or failure (under questioning) to account for his presence at a particular place, or failure to give evidence or answer questions at trial. In *Murray v UK* (1996) 22 E.H.R.R. 29 the ECtHR considered legal advice crucial to a defendant who exercised his right of silence. (This implies that the English provision, under the 1994 Act, requires a lawyer's presence in interrogation, before the court may apply an adverse inference.) In *Condron v UK* (2001) 31 E.H.R.R. 1, the ECtHR held, applying art.6, that it was inappropriate to draw an adverse inference, under the **1994 Act**, where defendants had maintained silence on their lawyer's advice. After a series of further cases, the jury instruction was rewritten twice. Judges complained in some cases that it was too favourable to the defendant. In *R. v Beckles* [2004] EWCA Crim 2766, the CA held that where a solicitor's advice was relied on, the jury should decide whether the facts relied on at trial were facts which the defendant could reasonably have been expected to mention at interview. If not, that is the end of the matter. It may still not have been reasonable for him to have relied on the advice, or the advice may have been the true explanation for his silence. Under the revised direction, the jury is asked to consider whether the defendant genuinely and reasonably relied on the advice to remain silent. See now *R. v Bresa* [2005] EWCA Crim 1414 and *R. v Hoare and Pierce* [2005] EWCA Crim 784. An adverse inference may not be drawn where the defendant refused to leave his cell for questioning: *R. v Johnson, R. v. Hind* [2005] EWCA Crim 971.

Mode of trial—Crown Court or magistrates' court?

KEY POINT

Indictable cases have to be tried in the Crown Court and summary offences in the magistrates' court but in the category of median seriousness, "triable either way", called "either way" cases, the magistrates may send a case up to the Crown Court, if they consider it too serious. If they have no preference, the defendant may elect to be dealt with by the Crown Court.

The RCCJ 1993 considered that many (expensive) Crown Court cases could more appropriately be dealt with in the (much cheaper) magistrates' court. It recommended removing the defendant's right to choose trial in the Crown Court and thus jury trial. While research had shown that the acquittal rate was higher in the Crown Court, in matched case, sentencing was harsher. The Home Office published a 1995 consultation paper on *Mode of Trial*, suggesting three options for resolving the problem that many trivial cases were sent up to the (expensive) Crown Court and given sentences within the magistrates' powers:

- classifying more offences as summary only;
- removing the defendant's right to elect; or
- requiring magistrates to ask defendants to indicate their plea before taking a decision on mode of trial.

The Government enacted the third option, in s.49 of the Criminal Procedure and Investigations Act 1996, known as the *plea before venue* procedure (now extended by the **Criminal Justice Act 2003**). The intention is that *magistrates will hear all either-way cases where the defendant indicates a guilty plea*, unless the magistrates consider their sentencing powers too low. Even before the section was brought into force, the 1997 Narey Report again suggested dispensing with the defendant's right to elect Crown Court trial and leaving trial venue to be determined by magistrates. In 1998, the Home Secretary published *Determining Mode of Trial in Either Way Cases-A Consultation Paper*. He set out the familiar arguments, as follows.

For abolition of the defendant's right to elect (Crown Court jury trial)

- The right only dated from 1855 and had nothing to do with **Magna Carta 1215**.
- 22,000 defendants chose Crown Court trial in 1997 but most changed their plea to guilty, after significant inconvenience and worry to witnesses and considerable extra cost.
- By definition, elected cases are those which magistrates have determined are suitable for them. The mode of trial decision should be based on objective assessment by the court of the gravity of the case, not the defendant's perception of what is advantageous to him.
- It was questionable whether defendants opted for jury trial to defend their reputation, as nine-tenths of those who did already had convictions.
- Most defendants elected jury trial because they wanted to delay proceedings, to apply pressure to the Crown to accept a guilty plea to a lesser offence, or to deter witnesses.
- Few other countries allowed the defendant a choice.

Arguments in favour of the right to elect jury trial

- The right helped to promote confidence in the criminal justice system.
- Whereas magistrates were concerned with the seriousness of the offence, it was the defendant's reputation which the public saw as justifying the right to elect.
- People usually defended the right because they would want jury trial if they were charged with something of which they were innocent.
- People assumed that Crown Court trial was fairer. Defendants mainly elected because they rightly believed they had a higher chance of acquittal.
- Some arguments went to merits of jury trial, for example, the jury's capacity to acquit contrary to legal proof of guilt, applying jury "equity", as discussed in the jury chapter.

The Home Secretary introduced the Criminal Justice (Mode of Trial) Bill in 1999, to abolish the right to elect and leave the decision to magistrates. It was condemned by the Bar, the Law Society, the Society of Black Lawyers and civil rights groups such as the Legal Action Group (LAG). Amongst other points, the LAG argued the following.

- Defendants usually opted for jury trial because they rightly saw their chances of obtaining justice in the Crown Court as significantly higher. In 1997, 62 per cent of defendants who pleaded not guilty to some or all counts were acquitted. Having a professional judge oversee the case was as important as having a jury. 54 per cent were acquitted because the judge discharged the case or directed an acquittal.
- Electing jury trial triggered other safeguards, such as greater prosecution disclosure.
- Removing the right would disadvantage black defendants. They more frequently chose the Crown Court.
- Other procedural changes would minimise defendants' manipulation of the system.

Wolchover and Heaton-Armstrong added the following, at (1998) 148 N.L.J. 1614 and see (2000) 150 N.L.J. 158.

- Defendants elected jury trial because it was inherently superior.
- Loss of liberty was no less serious for an habitual thief than loss of good name for someone with no previous convictions.

Courtney Griffiths Q.C. (*Counsel*, April 1999) added these points.

- Research by the Runnymede Trust, 1990, showed that, whereas under one third of white defendants, given the option, elected for jury trial, 45 per cent of black defendants elected.

- This was an intelligent choice. Only two per cent of magistrates were (then) non-white. Home Office research showed white defendants had a substantially better chance of being granted bail and were less likely to receive immediate custodial sentences than blacks.

A number of commentators emphasised that jury trial was inherently superior to summary trial.

- Listing for Crown Court trial triggered a much more careful review of the evidence by the CPS, which often resulted in their dropping the case or reducing the charges. This implied that, if magistrates were to decide on mode of trial, they would be doing so on inadequate information.
- At the Crown Court, a professional judge reviewed the strength and admissibility of the evidence, whereas magistrates were both fact-finders and arbiters of the law.

Nigel Ley ((1999) 149 N.L.J. 1316) drew attention to

- the fact that magistrates did not take notes of evidence or give reasons,
- that defendants in theft cases were often refused legal aid and
- solicitors in magistrates' courts were often ignorant of the law, as were magistrates' clerks. (Magistrates do give brief reasons now, because it is required by art.6 of the HR Convention).

Some critics pointed out that

- magistrates' courts are seen as police courts, and/or
- magistrates are considered part of the Establishment and they are not as socially and ethnically diverse as the jury.

This first Bill was heavily defeated in the House of Lords, in 2000. The Home Secretary replaced it with another, which was again defeated in 2000.

Auld L.J., in the Criminal Courts Review 2001, again recommended that magistrates should decide on the allocation of either-way cases, subject to an appeal to a district judge (magistrates' courts). This again attracted ferocious opposition from the legal profession and others, repeating the arguments above, so by the time it wrote its 2002 White Paper *Justice for All*, the Government had abandoned the idea and instead announced that it would increase magistrates' sentencing powers (thus by other means achieving their aim of shifting more work down to the magistrates' court).

The Government also introduced provisions in the **Criminal Justice Act 2003** to change the mode of trial decision-making procedure yet again, with a view to making the decisions of both magistrates and defendant better informed. These followed the recommendations in the Criminal Courts Review. The Act provides that, before deciding on mode of trial, the magistrates should be told of the defendant's previous convictions (Sch.3). They must give prosecution and defence a chance to air their views and take account of allocation guidelines issued by the *Sentencing Guidelines Council*, under s.170 of the **Criminal Justice Act 2003**. If the court decides the case is suitable for summary trial, it must explain so, in ordinary language, to the defendant and tell him he can choose a Crown Court trial but that, if the charge is of a certain violent or sexual offence, it can still commit him to the Crown Court for sentence if, having tried the case, it thinks its sentencing powers are too low. The defendant can then request an indication of the sentence he might get if he were to plead guilty in the magistrates' court but the court is not obliged to provide this. If it does, it must allow the defendant an opportunity to reconsider his plea. If it decides to send him to the Crown Court, or he elects a Crown Court trial, it must transfer him direct, under s.51 of the **Crime and Disorder Act 1998**, without a committal.

Committal proceedings
Almost all defendants in the Crown Court used to be committed for trial by magistrates, whose job it was to certify that there was a *prima facie* case against them. Mostly, this was a swift, paper exercise. It was abolished for indictable offences by s.51 of the **Crime and Disorder Act 1998**. The magistrates may transfer defendants directly to the Crown Court and, as explained above, this has been extended to either-way offences by the **Criminal Justice Act 2003**. Note: this has not yet been implemented so either way offences going to the Crown Court still have to be committed by the magistrates.

Pre-trial disclosure of evidence
Requirements for pre-trial disclosure had become more demanding since 1981, when the A.G. had generally required the prosecution to make available to the defence all unused material. The picture became more complex after miscarriages of justice were exposed in the early 1990s. Courts found it difficult to balance the defendant's interest in seeing all the evidence gathered and the prosecution's interest in keeping sensitive material (such as the identity of an informant). The RCCJ 1993 recommended a statutory scheme of disclosure. It was anxious to stop "ambush defences", where an unpredictable defence is raised at trial. This was effected by ss.34–39 of the **Criminal Justice and Public Order Act 1994**, which qualify the defendant's right of silence (see below).

The **Criminal Procedure and Investigations Act 1996**, Pt I, enacted a statutory scheme of disclosure for Crown Court cases. The prosecutor had a two-stage duty to disclose to the defence all unused material that might, in his opinion, undermine the prosecution case. The accused could give a written defence statement, in order to obtain secondary disclosure. If he did not do so he risked the judge inviting the jury to draw a negative inference from his failure. The **1996 Act** was criticised as allowing the prosecutor to choose what to disclose and for punishing the accused for not making a defence statement, thus eroding the principle of innocence until guilt is proven. In practice, defence statements were criticised as being so vague they were useless. (They were usually a couple of sentences.)

Auld L.J. examined these criticisms at length in the Criminal Courts Review 2001. Consequently, the Government amended the 1996 Act in the **Criminal Justice Act 2003**. The Act (Pt 5) replaces the old two-stage test with a single objective test, requiring the prosecutor to disclose material that has not previously been disclosed and which might reasonably be considered capable of undermining the case for the prosecution against the accused, or of assisting the case for the accused. It replaces the secondary disclosure stage with a revised continuing duty on the prosecutor to disclose material that meets the new test. The prosecutor is specifically required to review the prosecution material on receipt of the defence statement and to make further disclosure if required under the continuing duty.

It also amends defence disclosure requirements. The accused must provide a more detailed defence statement, setting out any particular defences on which he intends to rely and indicating any points of law he wishes to take, including any points as to the admissibility of evidence or abuse of process. The judge must warn the accused about any failure to comply with the defence statement requirements, because the judge may still invite the jury to draw an adverse inference if the defence statement is inadequate. An updated defence statement may be required to assist the management of the trial, requiring the accused to serve details of his witness and experts. The judge has the discretion to disclose the defence statement to the jury. The CPS and the police devised Joint Operational Instructions on disclosure, in response to a review by the CPS Inspectorate, in 2000. The A.G. also issues guidelines on disclosure, which are on her website. In 2006, the CA issued *A Protocol for the Control and Management of Unused Material for the Crown Court*. It called for a culture change, arguing that prosecutors should stop the practice of allowing the defence to inspect all unused material. It was the *prosecutor's* duty to inspect everything. Judges should inspect the defence statement to ensure that it complied with the statutory requirement.

The Plea

In common law countries, once the accused has pleaded guilty, the prosecutor does not need to prove the case, by bringing evidence and examining witnesses. There is no trial. Once the court accepts a guilty plea, the defendant is "proved guilty according to law", under art. 6 (2): *Revitt v DPP and joined cases* [2006] EWHC 2266 (Admin). In England and Wales, as in most common law jurisdictions, well over 90 per cent of defendants plead guilty. Following a guilty plea, there is a brief court appearance in either the magistrates' court or the Crown Court, depending on seriousness. The prosecution present a brief version of their case, "the facts", as they always call it; the accused may then make a plea in mitigation of sentence, asking for certain factors to be taken into account to lessen his sentence, then the magistrates or judge will sentence him. They may adjourn sentencing to require a pre-sentence or psychiatric report on the offender.

Plea bargaining

This means that the accused agrees to plead guilty in exchange for:

* an offer of a lower sentence;
* a reduction in charge to a less serious offence (charge bargaining); or
* a promise by the prosecution to present a less serious version of the facts (fact bargaining).

The first, well-known and widely used in the US, was generally impracticable here because judges could not take part in it, under the old rules laid down in *Turner* [1970] 2 Q.B. 321 and because prosecutors cannot generally recommend sentences, unlike American prosecutors, who routinely do deals over plea and sentence with the defence. *R. v Turner*, affirmed by a 1976 Practice Direction, held that counsel could advise the defendant (how to plead) in strong terms, provided he made it clear that the defendant had a free choice. Generally, the judge should "never indicate the sentence which he is minded to impose" and never indicate he would impose a severer sentence following a not guilty plea. He could not indicate that, having read the papers, he would impose a certain type of sentence, following a guilty plea. A judge was permitted to say that, whatever the plea, the sentence would take a particular form.

Nevertheless, there was persistent concern about the resources wasted by defendants pleading not guilty then changing their plea at the last minute, after an expensive Crown Court trial had been prepared (called a "cracked trial"). Some judges rewarded defendants with a sentence discount of up to one third in exchange for an early guilty plea, but practice was diverse and, historically, magistrates did not give sentencing discounts. Successive governments were concerned, in the 1990s, to stop the waste caused by cracked trials. The RCCJ 1993 recommended that the system of rewarding defendants for pleading guilty should be formalised. The earlier the guilty plea, the higher the sentence discount. Judges should be permitted to indicate, in advance of trial, the highest sentence they were prepared to give. Only the first part of the recommendation was enacted, in s.48 of the **Criminal Justice and Public Order Act 1994** (now repeated in the **Criminal Justice Act 2003**, ss.144 and 174). This puts a duty on the court, in sentencing a guilty pleader, to take into account the stage at which he pleaded guilty, and to announce in open court any resultant sentence reduction. This, of course, simply formalises the existing practice of rewards for early guilty pleas.

In his 2001 Criminal Courts Review, Auld L.J. reiterated the RCCJ's 1993 call for a formalised system of graduated sentencing discounts for guilty pleas, coupled with a system of advanced indication of sentence. The Government responded that it intended to introduce a clearer tariff of sentence discount. This is not incorporated in the **Criminal Justice Act 2003** but was announced by Lord Chancellor Falconer in 2003, as part of the Case Preparation Project (see below).

KEY POINT

The **Sentencing Guidelines Council** (SGC) published guidelines (on its website) on a graduated structure of sentence discounts for guilty pleas, to be applied in the Crown Court from 2005. A maximum one-third discount should be given to those who plead guilty at the earliest opportunity, in the police station. Those found guilty after a not guilty plea and trial get no discount. The sliding scale applied even if the defendant was caught red-handed. In *R. v Goodyear (Practice Note)* [2005] EWCA Crim 888, a five-judge CACD laid down what judges should do in this "different culture". They re-emphasised that the defendant's plea must be made voluntarily and free from improper pressure but this did not preclude the defendant from seeking an *advance indication of sentence*. They laid down guidelines:

- The judge should confine himself to indicating the maximum sentence for a guilty plea at that point.
- He could only act at the request of the defendant, not on his own initiative, or that of the defence lawyer.
- He could refuse a sentence indication but, once given, it was binding on him and other judges.
- A hypothetical indication should be refused.
- A judge should not be invited to give an indication on the basis of a plea bargain.
- He should not be asked to indicate levels of sentence dependent on different pleas.
- The defence advocate was responsible for ensuring that his client appreciated that he should not plead guilty unless he was guilty and that any sentence indication remained subject to the AG's right to appeal against an unduly lenient sentence.

Although these guidelines warn judges not to participate in plea bargaining, the system of rewarding people for guilty pleas by offering sentence discounts inevitably results in bargaining between prosecution and defence. Some find this practice offensive and dangerous, not least because some innocent people are persuaded to plead guilty and because those who exercise their right to trial are punished with a sentence 50 per cent heavier than those who confess at the police station and because giving people a sentence discount when they are caught red-handed destroys the system of just deserts. It was this last objection that led to public outcry in the summer of 2006, when judges were targeted by the *Sun* newspaper for passing lenient sentences on violent offenders and paedophiles (and announcing that the offender's sentence would normally be cut by parole, early release, and so on). The Home Secretary, John Reid, joined in the criticism until it was pointed out to him that his own department devised the parole rules and that judges had felt obliged to follow the Sentencing Guidelines Council's discount scheme. One case was referred to the CACD by the AG. The CACD said that the trial judge had been correct in applying the one-third discount: *Attorney General's Refs Nos 14 and 15 of 2006 (Tanya French and Alan Robert Webster)* [2006] EWCA Crim 1335. The SGC urgently reviewed the Guidelines, following consultation, especially in relation to cases like this, where people are caught red-handed and the prosecution case is so overwhelming that they have no grounds for pleading not guilty. In such cases, only a 20 per cent discount need be given.

The Serious Organised Crime and Police Act 2005, ss. 71–75 introduced a type of statutory, formalised plea bargaining. The Serious Organised Crime Agency (SOCA) can offer an offender contractual immunity from prosecution and a reduction in sentence in exchange for assistance in investigation and prosecution. The CA gave guidelines in *R. v P* [2007] EWCA Crim 2290. Additionally, it has been common practice in any type of serious case to offer immunity or sentence discounts to suspects who are prepared to give prosecution evidence and the courts have upheld these bargains by giving astonishingly big discounts of up to two thirds off a sentence. This contractual bargaining is sinister, to those of us who are concerned that we are importing American-style plea bargaining. The AG, exasperated with the collapse of so many expensive fraud trials, such as the Jubilee Line trial, discussed in the jury chapter, has been planning ways of persuading more people to plead guilty, rather than risking expensive jury trials, where the jury might well acquit or the trial collapse. Following the government's 2006 *Fraud Review*, she consulted in 2008 on offering binding pre-trial bargains, as above. Lake warns that it seems to have been forgotten that we have already tried offering witness immunity from prosecution, in the Northern Irish "supergrass" system, to obtain evidence against terrorists in "the troubles". Hundreds of convictions were overturned because the system was perceived to be open to abuse. Obviously, the convicted individual could argue that the witness whose evidence convicted them was unreliable, since they were bribed to give evidence with a promise of freedom: (2006) 156 N.L.J. 908.

Trial by judge alone
In the magistrates' court, a defendant may be dealt with by a bench of lay magistrates or a district judge (magistrates' court) sitting alone. He has no choice. In the Crown Court, following recommendations by Auld L.J., the **Criminal Justice Act 2003,** s.44 allows the judge to direct a judge-only trial where he is satisfied that there is a "real and present danger that jury tampering would take place". See jury chapter.

KEY POINT

The Act would have permitted the prosecution to apply for a judge-only trial in long or complex fraud trials **but the Government never implemented this,** promising to reconsider, as it was bitterly opposed in and out of Parliament. Following the collapse of the expensive Jubilee Line fraud trial, the Government attempted to reintroduce this measure, in the Fraud (Trials Without a Jury) Bill 2006–07 but it was defeated. This is explained further, in the jury chapter.

In 2002, the Law Commission suggested a two-stage procedure to prosecute multiple offences and this resulted in s.13 of the Domestic Violence, Crime and Victims Act 2004. If the jury convicts on a sample count, the other counts may be tried by judge alone. Some critics accused the government of sneaking in non-jury trials in a fairly obscure Act.

Case management hearings in the Crown Court
Since 1995 a plea and directions hearing, now called a plea and case management hearing (**Criminal Procedure Rules,** Pt 15), may be arranged prior to trial. This is very brief, designed to prepare for the trial and fix a trial date. In all class 1 or serious or complex cases, the prosecution provides a summary, identifying issues of law and fact and estimating trial length. The accused is arraigned and his plea entered. Following a not guilty plea, the parties are expected to inform the court of witnesses and any special requirements for trial. If the plea is guilty, the judge should, if possible, proceed to sentence, after hearing a plea in mitigation. Where the judge is considering a custodial sentence or non-custodial alternative, he may require a pre-sentence report or, where appropriate, a psychiatric or medical report. Many such oral hearings are now being replaced by virtual hearings or disposed of altogether, as the **2005 Rules** and the Effective Trial Management Programme leave it to the Case Progression Officer to monitor

trial preparation and communicate with the parties about timetabling. It is up to the lawyers to certify that the case is ready for trial.

Pre-trial hearings in the Crown Court

These are not new but were put onto a statutory footing by Pts III and IV of the **Criminal Procedure and Investigations Act 1996**. Prior to swearing-in the jury, the judge may order a preparatory hearing for one of the following purposes: identifying important issues; assisting the jury's comprehension of those issues; expediting proceedings; or assisting the judge's trial management. She may hear arguments and rule on points of law and admissibility of evidence. She may require detailed case statements and require the prosecution evidence and any explanatory material to be prepared in a form which she considers is likely to help the jury understand it.

Speeding up justice in the magistrates' court and Crown Court

Most recommendations of the 1997 Narey Report were enacted in the **Crime and Disorder Act 1998**. The magistrates' courts where the reforms were piloted cut the disposal time of all offenders by around two-thirds. Here are the main points.

- CPS staff were placed in police stations to advise on charges and non-lawyers were permitted to prosecute in the magistrates' court, as mentioned above.
- Early first hearings for straightforward guilty pleas were introduced in magistrates' courts.
- Early administrative hearings were introduced in contested cases.
- Case management powers were given to clerks and single magistrates.
- A Youth Justice Board, Youth Offending Teams and a set of new procedures were created, to speed up and co-ordinate the processing, treatment and rehabilitation of young offenders.

In its 2002 White Paper, *Justice for All*, the Government expressed the aim to make trials faster. From 2003, it published performance tables for the 42 criminal justice areas. Lord Falconer L.C. announced the Case Preparation Project, with Case Progression Officers, and this eventually resulted in the case management procedure prescribed by the **Criminal Procedure Rules 2005**, above. Very controversially, lawyers have been given financial incentives for early and proper preparation of cases, and defendants, as we have seen, are rewarded with graduated sentence discounts for earlier guilty pleas. Defendants who fail to attend lawyers' appointments may be imprisoned for breach of bail conditions.

The Ministry of Justice introduced a *simple, speedy summary justice system* for magistrates' courts, from about 2003, but researchers have questioned its claims of success. In 2006, the House of Commons Public Accounts Committee said that, in 2004–5, just under two thirds of magistrates' court trials and over a quarter of pre-trial hearings did not proceed, wasting £173 million of taxpayers, money. The government's latest tactics to save money are to allow the police to issue fixed penalty notices on the street for public order offences, thus reducing the number of people processed by the magistrates' court and in 2008–9, they are experimenting with virtual hearings from the police station, where the offender "appears" in the magistrates' court via a TV link from the police station and is dealt with by magistrates immediately.

THE CRIMINAL AND CIVIL TRIAL PROCESS

Trials occur in a tiny fraction of cases. Over 90 per cent of defendants to criminal charges plead guilty and thus appear in court only to offer a plea in mitigation and to be sentenced. In the civil courts, most cases are settled by negotiation between the parties, or judgment is entered in default, because the defendant has not entered a defence. There are significant differences between civil and criminal trials, such as the degree of proof required, and evidential differences, such as the rule against hearsay. The adversarial model cannot apply as well to criminal trials as it does to civil because the defendant is faced with such a powerful opponent, the state.

The judge as arbiter
Essentially, the judge acts as an unbiased umpire whose job it is to listen to evidence presented by both sides, without interfering in the preparation of the case, or the presentation of evidence or arguments (legal or factual) at trial. This is often contrasted with the role of European investigating magistrates, or the Scottish procurator fiscal who may direct criminal investigations, cross-examine the defendant and collect evidence for the trial court. There is no English equivalent. The judge does not normally summon witnesses and must generally leave the examination of witnesses, in court, to the parties. In *Jones v National Coal Board* [1957] 2 Q.B. 55 Lord Denning M.R. summarised the judge's role in the trial hearing. The judge should:

- listen to all the evidence, only interfering to clarify neglected or obscure points;
- see that advocates behave and stick to the rules;
- exclude irrelevancies and discourage repetition;
- make sure he or she understands the advocates' points; and
- at the end, make up his mind where the truth lies. (In a criminal trial and rare civil trials, this is the job of the magistrates or jury.)

If a judge interferes unduly in the conduct of a trial, the decision may be quashed because of a breach of the rules of natural justice (fair trial). Though judges leave it to the parties to present evidence, specialist judges, such as those of the Commercial or Admiralty Court, are appointed because of their expertise and are expected to use it. If an advocate forgets a vital precedent in legal argument, the judge can invite argument on it. The rule of non-intervention does not apply in some instances, as below.

- Where legal argument is addressed to the judge: judges are often in a dialogue with lawyers, especially in the appeal courts.
- In small claims in the county court most parties are unrepresented and need considerable help from the judge. The **Civil Procedure Rules 1998** permit the judge to choose appropriate procedure.
- Where a defendant is unrepresented, mostly in the magistrates' courts and in frequently in all civil courts, he is dependent on the good will and expertise of the Bench and clerk to help him put his case and examine witnesses and explain what is being asked of him.

The role of the magistrates' clerk (legal adviser)

In magistrates' court trials, the clerk (legal adviser) has an important role set down in case law, statute and Practice Directions. Magistrates are wholly dependent on their clerks for advice on law, practice, procedure and sentencing. The court clerk, by far the most prevalent legal adviser to magistrates, enjoyed no legal recognition whatever in this role until the enactment of s.117 of the **Courts and Legal Services Act 1990**. The justices' clerk's advisory role is set out in the **Courts Act 2003**, s.28. It "declares" his functions to include giving advice to justices, on request, about law, practice and procedure and empowers him to draw their attention to these matters at any time. See also the **Consolidated Criminal Practice Direction** and the Justices' Clerks Rules 2005.

The adversarial method of eliciting testimony

The parties are kept to a fixed order of speeches, in the question and answer method.

1. Prosecution (criminal trial) or claimant (civil trial) makes his opening speech.
2. His first witness is examined by him or his legal representative. In civil cases, under the **Civil Procedure Rules 1998**, a pre-trial witness statement normally serves as his evidence-in-chief. Undisputed testimony in civil and criminal cases may be admitted as a statement.
3. This witness is then cross-examined by the opposition.

4. Each witness is so examined until the end of the prosecution/ claimant's case.

5. At this point, the defence may invite the judge to decide that there is "no case to answer", because insufficient evidence has been brought to prove the case. It is up to the person bringing the case to prove it, not up to the defence to disprove it, generally speaking. In criminal trials, the **Criminal Justice Act 2003** Pt 9 introduced a facility for the prosecution to appeal against a judge's ruling of no case to answer or any other evidentiary ruling in which the judge has terminated the trial.

6. The defendant is examined by the defence advocate then cross-examined by the prosecution/claimant. In civil trials, see 2 above.

7. All the defence witnesses are so questioned.

8. The defence sum up.

9. The claimant/prosecution may reply.

10. In a Crown Court jury trial, the judge sums up the evidence for the jury and directs them on law.

11. In any jury trial, criminal or civil, the jury deliberate in secret. In a criminal trial, if the jury cannot reach a unanimous verdict (12–0), then the judge may permit a majority verdict (11–1 or 10–2) and failing any agreement, the jury are called a "hung jury" and the case must be dismissed but a retrial may be ordered.

12. In a civil case, if the judge (or, rarely, jury) finds the case proven "on the balance of probabilities", he must find for the claimant and make an order, normally in damages. In a criminal case, if the magistrates', or DJMC, or jury, find guilt proven "beyond reasonable doubt" they must convict the defendant. The defendant may then be sentenced by the magistrates or DJMC in the magistrates' court, or the judge in the Crown Court.

13. If the criminal case is not proven, the defendant is found "not guilty" and acquitted and is discharged. If the civil case is not proven, the judge dismisses it and may order costs against the unsuccessful claimant.

This strict order of proceedings is meant to guarantee "fair play". In criminal trials, each witness stays outside until called, so they cannot copy a previous witness, and the witness is strictly kept to answering the questions put. If he tries to add points, or pass an opinion, he is quickly stopped by the judge or advocates. This results in two problems.

- If the witness feels he has vital evidence to add, he has no way of volunteering it. This can be especially frustrating to expert witness, examined by non-experts. The RCCJ 1993 recommended that where expert evidence is disputed in criminal trials, the judge should invite the expert witness to say whether they wish to add to their evidence.

- This system is dependent on the expertise of the advocate, to bring out all and only that relevant information helpful to his case.

Advocates are not allowed to "lead" their witnesses, i.e. ask questions which suggest an answer, unless the judge and opposition consent. The very aim of cross-examination is, however, to mislead.

THE CRIMINAL TRIAL

The defendant is provided with certain safeguards in the criminal trial, to restore the balance slightly against the heavy weight of the state. The criminal quantum (standard) of proof is "beyond reasonable doubt", so it is much harder to prove a criminal case than a civil one, where the case must be proven "on the balance of probabilities". The accused has a right of silence though there have been inroads into this since 1994, as explained above. Certain evidence is excluded because it is unduly prejudicial against the defendant, inherently unreliable, or its utterance is against the public interest. Auld L.J. concluded, in his 2001 Review, however, that we should move away from the strict rule against the admission of certain evidence in criminal proceedings, to a more flexible position where we admit such evidence and instead trust fact-finders to assess the weight of the evidence. The Government agreed with him in the White Paper, *Justice for All* (2002). Accordingly, the **Criminal Justice Act 2003** modifies certain of these exclusory rules and we can expect further such modifications to the law of criminal evidence. Below are some examples of evidence which is generally excluded.

1. *Defendant's previous convictions*, with certain exceptions. Following recommendations by the Law Commission and Auld L.J., the **Criminal Justice Act 2003** (in ss.98–113) replaces all common law and statutory provisions with a comprehensive set of rules for the admissibility of previous misconduct evidence in respect both of witnesses and defendants.
2. *Communications between client and legal adviser*, without permission.
3. *Hearsay evidence*: the basic rule against hearsay was that evidence could not be related to the court unless its author was there to present it. It applied to the related spoken word and documents. It was thought to be inherently unfair to rely on the evidence of a witness who was not present to be cross-examined. The hearsay rule was subject to so many exceptions that it was very difficult to apply, in practice. It was abolished in civil cases by the Civil Evidence Act 1995. The RCCJ 1993 recommended that hearsay be admitted more frequently in criminal trials. The Law Commission reported on this in 1997 and the hearsay rule was again considered by

Sir Robin Auld in the Criminal Courts Review 2001. He concluded that we should move away from the strict rule to a more flexible position where we admit such evidence and trust the fact-finders (magistrates or jury) to assess its importance. Sections 114–136 of the **Criminal Justice Act 2003** are intended to codify hearsay law. They remove the old common law rule against the admission of hearsay evidence and provide that such evidence will be admissible (on behalf of the prosecution and defence) provided certain safeguards are met. The Act provides the court with an additional statutory discretion to allow an out-of-court statement where all parties agree to admission or it is satisfied that it is in the interests of justice for it to be admitted. Witnesses' previous statements are now more widely admissible at trial (as proof of the facts contained within), including allowing certain witnesses in serious cases to use their video-recorded statements in place of their main evidence.

4. *Confessions obtained by oppression* or in consequence of anything said or done which, in the circumstances, rendered the confession unreliable. The burden of proving that a confession was not so obtained is on the prosecution (Police and Criminal Evidence Act 1984, s.76).

5. *Unfairly obtained evidence* (**Police and Criminal Evidence Act 1984**, s.78).

YOUNG OFFENDERS

The age of criminal responsibility is 10. As mentioned above, most 10–17 year old young offenders are cautioned by the police, following an admission of guilt. For those who are prosecuted, almost all are dealt with in the youth court, a court using a mixed gender bench or a district judge (magistrates' courts) (DJMC) in the magistrates' court. The public are excluded. Journalists may report proceedings but not identify the young defendant or witnesses. Procedure is informal, normally without fixed court furniture. The magistrates or DJMC address the defendant by first name and parents or guardians may accompany the child. Magistrates' disposal powers are different from those relating to adult offenders. Young offenders may only be sent for trial in the Crown Court if certain statutory conditions are satisfied, such as those under Sch.3 of the Criminal Justice Act 2003. For example, magistrates must send the following to the Crown Court.

- Children charged with murder, manslaughter or firearms offences.
- Children charged with adults.
- Children convicted in the Crown Court, where the magistrates' court feels that they deserve a greater sentence than they can apply.

This is not a complete list. Rose L.J. described the procedure for determining a young person's mode of trial "labyrinthine".

For those tried in the Crown Court, the ECtHR has ruled that the normal adult trial is too intimidating and incomprehensible for a child and a breach of art. 6: *T. and V. v UK* [2000] 2 All E.R. 1024. Consequently, the **Consolidated Criminal Practice Direction,** Pt IV says that youth trials must be conducted in accordance with the age, maturity and development of the defendant. Robes, wigs and police uniform should not normally be worn, the participants should be on the same level, the defendant should be able to sit near family or guardians and should be given frequent breaks, and so on.

The youth justice system is overseen by the Youth Justice Board and more details are on its website.

CRIMINAL APPEALS

As can be seen from the following description, there is no logic in our appeals system. For an excellent, thought-provoking examination of the system and the potential aims of appeals, see J. Spencer, "Does Our Present Criminal Appeal System Make Sense?" [2006] Crim. L.R. 677. Se also Law Commission Consultation Paper No 184.

Appeals from the magistrates' court
Appeals to the Crown Court

A defendant may appeal, as of right, on fact or law and against sentence and/ or conviction. The appeal is a complete rehearing by a circuit judge or recorder and two to four magistrates. The Crown Court may:

- correct any mistake in the order or judgment;
- confirm, reverse or vary the decision;
- remit the matter, with its opinion, to the magistrates; and
- make any order it thinks just and exercise any power of the magistrates' court. Thus, it may increase a sentence, within the magistrates' maxima.

Appeals to the High Court by way of case stated

Any prosecutor or defendant, aggrieved by the magistrates' decision, may, if they consider it wrong in law or in excess of jurisdiction, apply to the magistrates to state a case for the opinion of the HC. The stated case is a statement of reasons for the decision drafted by the magistrates' clerk (legal adviser). These appeals are heard by the Divisional Court of the Queen's Bench Division who may:

- reverse, affirm or amend the decision;
- remit it to the magistrates, with an opinion; or
- make such other orders as it thinks fit, including directing the magistrates to convict or acquit.

The QBD may also be asked to judicially review the magistrates' court proceedings on the ground of procedural impropriety, unfairness or bias, though the QBD has said it prefers the case stated procedure to be used. A further appeal, subject to leave, is permitted to the UKSC, as below.

Appeals from the Crown Court to the Court of Appeal (Criminal Division)
Appeal against conviction

Under the Criminal Appeal Act 1995, s.1, the convicted defendant may appeal if he has either:

- a certificate from the trial judge that the case is fit for appeal; or
- leave (permission) of the CA.

Single HC judges consider written applications for leave. Applicants have around a 25 per cent chance of success. Where leave is refused, the judge may order that time spent in custody after lodging the appeal should not count towards sentence. This is to discourage frivolous appeals, which burden the lists and delay meritorious appeals. The CA's powers are set out in the Criminal Appeal Act 1968, which has been substantially amended by the **1995 Act**. This section sets out the amended version of the **1968 Act** and then explains the background to the **1995 Act**.

The power of the CA to admit fresh evidence

Under s.23 (1) and (3) of the 1968 Act, as amended by the **1995 Act**, the CA may, *"if they think it necessary or expedient in the interests of justice"*,

(i) order the production of any *document*, exhibit or other thing connected with the proceedings;
(ii) order the examination of any *witness* who would have been a compellable witness at the trial, whether or not he or she was called; and
(iii) receive any *evidence* which was not adduced in the proceedings from which the appeal lies.

In considering whether to receive evidence, the CA must have regard in particular to:

"(a) whether the evidence appears to the court to be *capable of belief*;

(b) whether it appears to the court that the evidence may afford any ground for allowing the appeal;

(c) whether the evidence would have been admissible in the proceedings from which the appeal lies on an issue which is the subject of the appeal; and

(d) whether there is a reasonable *explanation* for the failure to adduce the evidence in those proceedings"

(**1968 Act**, s.23(2), as substituted by s.4 of the **1995 Act**—my emphasis). The CA has held itself to be free to admit evidence irrespective of these criteria: *R. v Bowler* [1997] EWCA Crim 1957.

Background

Under the old law (pre-1995), the CA had a duty to admit fresh evidence where it was not available at the original trial, under prescribed conditions, and a wider power to admit it if it thought it necessary or expedient in the interests of justice. Its reluctance to admit fresh evidence was repeatedly criticised by the pressure group JUSTICE and by the producers of the television series *Rough Justice* and authors of the book of the same name, all of which focused on alleged miscarriages of justice. The CA required a particular type of explanation as to why evidence was not called at the time of trial, such as that it was not available. If it was available but simply not called, owing to, say, defence lawyers' negligence, prosecution's obstructiveness or a shortfall of legal aid, then this apparently would not suffice as an explanation acceptable to the CA. In many of these cases it took a "trial by television" and a reference by the Home Secretary to reopen the case. The House of Commons Home Affairs Committee in the early 1980s, then JUSTICE in 1989, and the RCCJ in 1993 urged the CA to take a broad approach to the question of whether fresh evidence was available at the time of the trial and, if it were, to the explanation why it was not adduced or why a witness had changed his story. The test for receiving fresh evidence, argued the RCCJ, should be whether it was "capable of belief". In fresh evidence cases, the CA should order a retrial unless impracticable, in which case it should decide the case itself.

In a 1994 consultation paper, the Home Office broadly agreed but thought the CA's power to exclude fresh evidence should be preserved, in cases where there was no reasonable explanation for the failure to produce it at trial. As you can see above, this is satisfied in the Act by the use of the word *may* in conjunction with its power to have regard to the explanation offered. In *Pendleton* [2001] UKHL 66, the leading case, the House of Lords said the correct test for the CA to apply was to consider the effect of the fresh evidence on the minds of the court, not the effect it would have had on a jury. In *R. v Gautier* [2007] All E.R. (D) 137, where the appellant sought to rely on a witness not called by the defendant's lawyer at the trial, the CA said it would not admit the new evidence unless there was a "lurking doubt", caused by flagrantly incompetent advocacy.

In *Hanratty* [2002] EWCA Crim 1141, the CA admitted fresh DNA evidence confirming the defendant's guilt, the reverse of the usual reason for admission. (He had been hanged for murder decades earlier). It held that its overriding consideration was to achieve justice.

Grounds for allowing and dismissing appeals

Section 2 of the **Criminal Appeal Act 1968**, as amended by the **1995 Act**, now provides that:
"Subject to the provisions of this Act, the Court of Appeal

(a)   *shall* allow an appeal against conviction if they think that the conviction is unsafe; and
(b)   *shall* dismiss such an appeal in any other case". (My emphasis).

Background

Under the unamended Act, the CA had the power to allow an appeal if it considered a jury's verdict "unsafe or unsatisfactory" or that there was an error of law or material irregularity in the course of the trial. Section 2 included a very important proviso which meant that the court could dismiss an appeal where, despite finding that something had gone wrong at the trial, it thought the defendant was, nevertheless, really guilty so that "no miscarriage of justice has actually occurred". The CA had been criticised for too readily using the proviso to uphold convictions where something had gone seriously wrong at the trial.

The RCCJ recommended that s.2 (1) of the **1968 Act** should be redrafted. It considered that the grounds overlapped and that there was confusion over the proviso. The grounds, it recommended, should be replaced by a single broad ground, giving the CA power to rule in any case where it felt a conviction "is or may be unsafe". The proviso would be redundant if the CA simply dismissed an appeal where it found an error had not rendered a conviction unsafe or ordered a retrial in those cases where it considered a conviction might be unsafe. This power would be exercisable regardless of there being no fresh evidence, no error in law and no material irregularity. It recommended that the CA should have an additional power to refer cases that require further investigation to a new body to be responsible for investigating alleged miscarriages of justice.

The Government broadly agreed with these proposals but notice that the CA now has to be satisfied that the verdict is *unsafe*. The Royal Commission's suggested words *or may be* were not included in the section. Critics have said that this is too restrictive on the CA's powers. Nevertheless in a 2006 paper, the Government considered whether to reintroduce a power in the CA to uphold a conviction where there was a clear technical error in the defendant's trial and conviction but where the court thought the person is really guilty, thus restoring the law to its pre-1995 position. The proposal was very heavily criticised. No judge or academic supported it because they were well aware of the unfairness of the old proviso, effectively allowing the CA to say "we think something went seriously wrong with your trial but we are going to uphold your conviction".

As well as the power to quash a conviction, the CA also has the power to order a retrial (discussed below) or convict for an alternative offence, or substitute a verdict of insanity or unfitness to plead.

The Court of Appeal's attitude towards its powers

Generally speaking, the CA was criticised pre-1995 for placing too restrictive an interpretation on its already limited powers. The main reason why the CA is so reluctant to overturn a conviction by a Crown Court jury is that, unlike the jury, it has not seen the witnesses and evidence first-hand. Further, it tends to revere the primacy of the jury, as the quotation below illustrates.

KEY POINT

It is important to understand that the CA does not provide a rehearing in criminal cases, unlike an appeal from a magistrates' court to the Crown Court. The limited powers of the CA were spelled out in the successful 1991 appeal of the Birmingham Six, *R. v McIlkenny* [1992] 2 All E.R. 417:

"Nothing in s.2 of the Act, or anywhere else obliges or entitles us to say whether we think that the appellant is innocent. This is a point of great constitutional importance. The task of deciding whether a man is innocent or guilty falls on the jury. We are concerned solely with the question whether the verdict of the jury can stand. Rightly or wrongly (we think rightly) trial by jury is the foundation of our criminal justice system . . . The primacy of the jury in the criminal justice system is well illustrated by the difference between the Criminal and Civil Divisions of the Court of Appeal . . . A civil appeal is by way of rehearing of the whole case. So the court is concerned with fact as well as law . . . It follows that in a civil case the Court of Appeal may take a different view of the facts from the court below. In a criminal case this is not possible . . . the Criminal Division is perhaps more accurately described as a court of review" (at 311).

The CA is continually swamped with criminal appeals and there are so many decisions on the meaning of "unsafe" that it is not possible to generalise. In *R. v A* [2001] UKHL 25, the HL held that a breach of Art.6 of the European Convention will always result in a conviction being unsafe. In *R. v Ashton* [2006] EWCA Crim 794 the CA took a very restricted attitude to allowing a conviction to be quashed where there had been a procedural failure but there was no real possibility that the prosecution or defence had been prejudiced by it. These cases follow a trend in which the court seems to be attempting to put a stop to people "getting off on a technicality". They shift concentration to the individual justice of a case. The CA sometimes allows an appeal on the rather vague old common law ground that they have a "lurking doubt" about the safety of a conviction. See Leigh at [2006] Crim. L.R. 809.

The power to order retrials

The **1968 Act**, s.7, as amended by the Criminal Justice Act 1988, provides that, where the CA allows an appeal against conviction, it may order that the appellant be retried where it appears that this is required in the interests of justice.

Appeals against sentence and A.G.'s references on sentence

The defendant may appeal from the Crown Court to the CA, which may substitute any other sentence or order within the powers of the Crown Court, provided it is not more severe than originally. The **Criminal Justice Act 1988**, s.36 gives the A.G. a power to refer any "unduly lenient" Crown Court sentence to the CA, which then has the power to increase it. The A.G. may then refer any such decision of the CA to the UK Supreme Court.

Prosecution appeals: Attorney General's References

The A.G. may, under the Criminal Justice Act 1972, refer an appeal, following an acquittal, to the CA and UKSC, on behalf of the prosecution. The appeal court simply clarifies the law, leaving the acquittal untouched.

Prosecution appeals against a trial judge's ruling

The **Criminal Justice Act 2003**, Pt 9 introduced a right of appeal to the CA by the prosecution against a judge's ruling (usually on a point of law or admissibility or strength of the evidence) which has terminated the trial (thus acquitting the accused) before a jury has been convened or during the prosecution case, or as a result of a submission of "no case to answer" by the defence, at the conclusion of the prosecution case. The Act also introduced a prosecution appeal against a judge's ruling which has been made at any time before the close of the prosecution case. In both instances, the prosecution must obtain leave from the trial judge or the CA. The CA may affirm the ruling and acquit the defendant, remit the case to the trial court for the trial to continue or order a retrial. This follows a recommendation by Auld L.J. in the Criminal Courts Review 2001, agreeing with recommendations of the Law Commission.

Prosecution applications to quash an acquittal

The **2003 Act**, Pt 10 also made a controversial exception to the double jeopardy rule, which protects a person from being tried twice for the same offence. With the DPP's consent, a prosecutor may apply to the CA to quash an acquittal (here or abroad) and order a retrial. If the CA is satisfied that there is "new and compelling evidence" (reliable, substantial and highly probative) against the acquitted person, in relation to the offence, and that it is in the interests of justice to do so, it *must* quash the acquittal and order a retrial. The provision applies only to serious offences such as rape, armed robbery, murder and manslaughter. This enactment follows a recommendation of Auld L.J. in the Criminal Courts Review. He, in turn, was influenced by this suggestion in the Macpherson Report on the Stephen Lawrence Inquiry, a recommendation of the House of Commons Home Affairs Select Committee and a Law Commission report. *R. v Dunlop* [2006] EWCA Crim 1354 was the first time the CA exercised this new power, quashing Dunlop's 1991 acquittal for the murder of Julie Hogg. He confessed to the murder in 1999. This case was well known and highly publicised at the time that Auld L.J. made his 2001 recommendation. Dunlop pleaded guilty at his retrial in 2006.

Appeals to the United Kingdom Supreme Court

Either prosecutor or defendant may appeal, with leave, to the UKSC, from an appeal hearing in the Divisional Court of the High Court QBD, on a *point of law of general public importance* (**Administration of Justice Act 1960**). This is called a "leapfrog" appeal, because the case by-passes the CA. Either prosecutor or defendant may appeal from the CA, provided the CA certifies that a point of law of general public importance is involved and that either court considers that the point should be considered by the UKSC and grants leave. The UKSC, in disposing of the appeal, may exercise any of the powers of the CA, or remit the case to it (**Criminal Appeal Act 1968**).

THE POST-APPEAL STAGE: RE-EXAMINING ALLEGED MISCARRIAGES OF JUSTICE

Where a person thinks he has been wrongly convicted by a jury or magistrates and he has lost an appeal or been refused leave to appeal, he may now seek the assistance of the independent Criminal Cases Review Commission (CCRC), or somebody else may petition them on his behalf. This is likely to be an MP, or a campaigning group, or an organisation such as JUSTICE. The CCRC was created by Pt II of the **1995 Act** and started work in 1997. Its 11 members are appointed for terms of five years. At least one third must be legally qualified.

1. The CCRC is empowered to refer Crown Court convictions and sentences to the CA and summary convictions and sentences (made by the magistrates' court) to the Crown Court.
2. It must "consider that there is a real possibility that the conviction, verdict, finding or sentence would not be upheld, were the reference to be made" because of argument or evidence not raised earlier. These conditions appear rather restrictive but these are followed by a broad power to make a reference "if it appears to the Commission that there are exceptional circumstances which justify making it".
3. It may not refer a conviction back to the CA just because the law has changed: **Criminal Justice and Immigration Act 2008**, s. 42.
4. It may be directed by the CA to investigate a case and
5. It may be asked by the Home Secretary to consider a matter arising in his consideration of whether to exercise the prerogative of mercy.
6. The CCRC has powers to obtain documents and may direct investigations by police officers or another public body.

Although the CCRC is a welcome replacement for the former arrangements for investigating alleged miscarriages of justice (a handful of Home Office civil servants), the CCRC's powers and approach have been criticised. Concern was expressed, before its creation, that the CCRC ought to have been provided with independent investigators. It has always had a backlog of thousands of cases awaiting investigation, which is not alleviated by its preparedness to spend time re-examining the cases of those long dead, such as Derek Bentley, James Hanratty and Ruth Ellis. Some critics, such as Duff, have said that the CCRC is preoccupied with trying to second guess the CA. He thinks they should more readily refer cases to the Home Secretary, in the hope that he will exercise his prerogative of mercy. For statistics and details of its caseload, see the CCRC website and for a debate on the success rate and working methods of the CCRC, see Nobles and Schiff's critique at [2005] Crim. L.R. 173 and reply by the then CCRC chair, Graham Zellick at [2005] Crim. L.R. 237.

The royal prerogative of mercy

The prerogative of mercy is the power to pardon convicted individuals as part of the residuary royal prerogative, exercised by the Crown on the advice of the Home Secretary, effectively, by civil servants. The prerogative is exercised in three ways:

(a)   A free pardon: quashing and expunging a conviction.
(b)   A conditional pardon: excusing or varying the conviction, subject to conditions, e.g. by commuting sentences.
(c)   Remission of a sentence.

General background to the Criminal Appeal Act 1995: widespread concern over miscarriages of justice

Prior to 1995, the Home Secretary had both a prerogative power of mercy, which he retains, and a statutory power to refer cases to the CA. The Home Secretary always used the prerogative to pardon sparingly, so as not to invoke the criticism of over-interference by the executive in the judicial function and because of the notion that the jury's verdict is sacrosanct. The House of Commons Home Affairs Committee complained in 1981 that the prerogative was used reluctantly. It recommended an independent review body and the RCCJ repeated that call.

The most famous miscarriages of justice in modern times are the cases of the Guildford Four and the Birmingham Six. The RCCJ was established to investigate the criminal justice process on the day the latter were released, in 1991. Concerns had, however, been raised for decades beforehand, over individuals who had allegedly been wrongfully imprisoned. Television programmes such as *Rough Justice* had alerted the public to the inadequacy of the appeal and post-appeal procedures. These are probably best summarised in a JUSTICE Report, *Miscarriages of Justice* (1989), known as the Waller Report. It is well worth reading and, below, I list the causes of injustice identified by their report, explaining, in square brackets, how these were later manifested in famous cases.

Pre-trial

1.   Poor work by defence lawyers.
2.   Cases involving poor police investigation and/or police misconduct. [The stories behind the Guildford Four and Birmingham Six involve a sad litany

of police corruption, notably of police brutality inducing false confessions. *Downing* [2002] EWCA Crim 263 was a case where a very vulnerable young person confessed after oppressive detention, as was that of Robert Brown, freed on appeal in 2002, after 25 years in prison and Stephan Kisko, who wrongly confessed to a murder after two days' questioning, without a lawyer and served 16 years of wrongful imprisonment.] The Waller Report recites psychiatric research which gives a fascinating insight into why people confess to crimes they did not commit but for more detail see G. Gudjonsson, *The Psychology of Interrogations and Confessions: A Handbook* (2002, Wiley).

Trial

3. Poor work by defence counsel: late briefs, bad trial tactics and failure to call witnesses.
4. Underhand tactics by the prosecution. [In the Guildford Four case, it was alleged that the police realised, early on, that they might not have caught the right people but they suppressed evidence in favour of the defence, such as an interview with an alibi witness.]
5. Poor summing up by the judge. [In the Guildford Four case, the summing up by the trial judge was acknowledged by the CA to be faulty but it did not consider it sufficient reason to allow leave to appeal. As for the Birmingham Six, the summing up by their trial judge (who later became a law lord) went overboard in indicating a guilty verdict.]

Appeal

6. Bad advice on appeal.
7. The majority of appeals are concerned with legal technicalities, not the guilt or innocence of the accused.
8. A reluctance to interfere with the trial verdict. [In the Birmingham Six case, the CA, headed by Lord Lane C.J., which heard the Six's 1987 appeal, was very heavily criticised for its refusal to overturn the jury's verdict, despite new evidence casting serious doubt on the convictions.]

Post-appeal

9. The desire of former Home Secretaries, as part of the executive government, not to be seen to be interfering with the work of the courts led them to ignore errors 1–7 above. [By the time the Home Secretary had referred the Birmingham Six's appeal back to the CA, the case had already been the subject of a book and a TV drama documentary, and opinion polls showed that most Americans, including President Bush senior and most Irish people, including their Prime Minister, assumed the Six to be innocent.]

10. Inadequate re-investigation by the police. [The police were criticised for taking two years to investigate the Guildford Four's convictions.]

Additionally, the above cases and later cases, such as those of Sally Clark and Angela Cannings in 2003, highlighted specific weaknesses in the system:

11. Inefficiency in forensic science services and inadequate services for the defence, as emphasised by the May Inquiry into the Guildford and Maguire cases.

12. Inadequate safeguards for defendants held under terrorist legislation. [Note: many commentators have said the injustices occurring in the Irish cases could not now be repeated, because of the **Police and Criminal Evidence Act 1984**. This is erroneous. Today, suspected terrorists are still held under different statutory powers.]

13. The danger of allowing the jury to convict on uncorroborated confession evidence.

14. Over-anxiety on the part of the police to secure a conviction, including a preparedness to fabricate evidence, in cases where there is a public outcry against the perpetrators. All these cases involve Irish or black defendants.

15. Over-willingness in certain CA judges, pre–1990, to believe prosecution evidence, probably caused by the fact that the majority of them were recruited from prosecuting counsel. This is not true now.

16. Limited powers of the CA: an inability to provide a full rehearing.

17. Failure to disclose exculpatory evidence and over-reliance on individual expert evidence [such as in Sally Clark's and Angela Cannings' convictions for murder after their babies died. After these two cases, the CA laid down guidance to prosecutors in cot death cases (*Cannings* [2004] EWCA Crim 1) and the A.G. reviewed over 258 convictions in similar cases. In his 2001 Review, Auld L.J. had expressed concern over the lack of regulation of experts. The A.G. has published guidance for experts and see *R. v B* (CA 2006)].

The effect of the Human Rights Act 1998 and the European Convention on Human Rights on criminal procedure

The **Human Rights Act 1998** gave "further effect" to the Convention and required courts and tribunals to take it into account in their proceedings (this permits them to re-interpret the law and read words into a statute). Since 2000, when it came into force, the Act's biggest area of impact has been criminal procedure, notably via arts 5 and 6, above. Defendants can make use of the Convention in various ways, such as a defence or to found an argument of "no case to answer", or as grounds of appeal. Below are some examples of the Convention's application. For an excellent two-page evaluation of the impact of the HRA on the criminal process see I. Dennis, Editorial: "Reconsidering the Human Rights Act" [2006] Crim. L.R. 577.

- Article 8 guarantees the right to private life, allowing interference only where necessary if national security and public safety are threatened, or in the prevention of crime and disorder. Surveillance methods, such as phone tapping and bugging must be prescribed by law, with a system of accountability. Liberty, the human rights organisation, and police organisations argue that this evidence should be used to try terrorist suspects, as it is throughout Europe, rather than detaining them in house arrest. Unusually, such evidence was used in the retrial of terrorists in 2009, convicted of plotting to blow up aircraft using bombs disguised as soft drinks. In 2009, the Home Office consulted on *Keeping the Right People on the DNA Database*, after the ECtHR ruled that the policy of indefinite retention of arrested people's fingerprints breached art.8

- Article 6(3)(c) (fair trial) grants the right to legal assistance to everyone charged with a criminal offence, where it is "necessary in the interests of justice"; this is the criterion for publicly-funded defence, set out in the **Access to Justice Act 1999**. The ECtHR has held that an accused's right to communicate in confidence with his lawyer is an essential element of art.6 (3)(c).

- In *SS for the Home Dept v AF and another* [2009] UKHL 28, the law lords ruled that the appellant's art.6 fair trial rights had been violated, as he had been the subject of a control order (house arrest), as a terror suspect, pursuant to the Terrorism Act 2005, s.2, for three years. The government sought non-disclosure of intelligence on which the house arrest was based. Rather than disclose the evidence and jeopardise other terror investigations, the Home Secretary lifted the order.

- The law and practice on bail had to be amended, to make it Convention-compliant, as explained above. Courts now need more substantial evidence on which to base their bail decisions, keep them under review, and they must keep in mind the presumption of innocence and give full reasons, not just "tick-box" reasons. Also, statute banning bail for certain suspects had to be amended as it breached the Convention.

- As explained above, in the section on the right of silence, after *Saunders* various statutes had to be amended by the Youth Justice and Criminal Evidence Act 1999 because they required a suspect to answer questions and thus fell foul of art.6.

- Critics said the statutory regime for disclosure under the **Criminal Procedure and Investigations Act 1996** fell foul of art.6 in various ways and it has now been amended in the **Criminal Justice Act 2003**, as explained above. Nevertheless, critics say the Act fails to remedy breaches of art.6 in public interest immunity cases, as exposed in *Edwards and Lewis v UK* [2003] Crim. L.R. 891.

- The ECtHR has held that a costs order against an acquitted defendant violates the presumption of innocence, under art.6 (2).

- The child murderers of Jamie Bulger took the UK Government to the ECtHR, alleging they had been denied a fair trial under art.6 (*T and V v UK* (2000) 30 E.H.R.R. 121). The Court agreed that the formality and ritual of the Crown Court trial must have been intimidating and incomprehensible to 11-year-old children. Consequently, Crown Court youth trial practice was reformed, as explained above.

- The Convention requires a reasoned decision. Nevertheless, in *Gregory v UK* (1998) 25 E.H.R.R. 577 the ECtHR held that the secrecy of jury deliberations did not render a trial unfair. Magistrates' courts are not courts of record. Historically this made appeals difficult. Magistrates now keep trial notes and give reasoned decisions.

- In *Sander v UK* (2001) 31 E.H.R.R. 44 the ECtHR ruled that the defendant's fraud trial had been in breach of art.6, because one of the jurors had warned the judge that the jury might not be impartial because some of them were making racist jokes.

- English and Welsh judges are extremely reluctant to allow handcuffs in court: art.3, prohibition of torture, inhuman or degrading treatment.

Revision Checklist

You need to appreciate the following points and understand any arguments surrounding them:

- the importance of the common law and **European Convention on Human Rights** as the basis for criminal procedure rules, and the relationship between them;

- the main case management elements and ethos of the **Criminal Procedure Rules 2005**;

- prosecutors and how the prosecution system works;

- how the bail system works and the grounds for refusing bail;

- how legislation has affected the right to silence, the controversy surrounding this, and how the European Court of Human Rights has ruled on this issue;

- how cases are allocated between the magistrates' court and the Crown Court and the arguments for and against retaining the defendant's right to choose the mode of trial;

- the rules of pre-trial disclosure and how these have been altered in 2003;

- the system of rewarding guilty pleas, unofficially called "plea bargaining"; how informal sentencing rewards have now been sanctioned by the law and how practice has now been set down by *Goodyear* and the Sentencing Guidelines Council;

- the pre-trial hearings that may take place, the basic pattern of civil and criminal trials and the special safeguards in the criminal trial;

- the system of criminal appeals and how this was reformed in the **Criminal Appeal Act 1995**;

- the system for dealing with alleged miscarriages of justice at the post-appeal stage and the common causes of miscarriages of justice; and

- the way in which the **European Convention on Human Rights** and its interpretation by the European Court of human Rights has impacted on criminal procedure and practice in England and Wales.

FURTHER READING/UPDATING

Darbyshire on the ELS (2008), Chapter 12, further reading listed therein and website updates
Archbold News (on *Westlaw*)
Criminal Law Review (on *Westlaw*)
New Law Journal
Legal Journals Index (on *Westlaw*)

websites
Attorney General
CJS Online
Criminal Courts Review
Crown Prosecution Service
HM Courts Service
Ministry of Justice, especially Criminal Procedure Rules and the Consolidated
Criminal Practice Direction
Youth Justice Board

QUESTION AND ANSWER

The Question

Priya is arrested for theft of a bar of chocolate from her local convenience store. (Theft is an "either way" offence). Explain what may happen to her and the choices that she may be faced with.

Advice and the Answer

Advice

This is a problem. Deal with the problem. Do not write all you know about criminal procedure or lapse into a discursive essay about it. Do not get bogged down in writing in detail about part of the procedure, because you need to provide a balanced account. Describe it in outline then expand as time allows. In an exam, leave a few lines before each point, to allow room for elaboration, or in case you remember something you have missed out.

Answer guide

1. If Priya admits her guilt to the police, she may be dealt with by an early intervention scheme or may be offered a caution, instead of prosecution. A caution will go on her criminal record. A caution is highly likely, if she is 10–17, since most offences committed by young offenders are disposed of by way of a caution, meaning a reprimand or final warning, under the **Crime and Disorder Act 1998**, unless she is a persistent offender. If she is an adult, she may still be offered a caution, or a conditional caution under the **CJA 2003**. A child or adult may be dealt with by a fixed penalty, imposed by the police. This does not form part of the offender's criminal record but police and courts do have access to records of fixed penalties.

2. In taking this important decision, she should be offered the assistance of the duty solicitor, or may apply for a solicitor of her choice, under the Criminal Defence Service (legal aid) scheme, if she cannot afford to pay privately. If she is a child, she will not be means tested. As a child or adult, her case will still have to satisfy the "interests of justice" test and she is more likely to satisfy it if she is a child because she will be less capable of representing herself.

3. If she is under 10, she is below the age of criminal responsibility and may not be treated as a criminal suspect, though the police will no doubt inform and warn her parent(s) or guardian(s). If an adult told her to steal, she is their innocent agent and they may be charged with theft.

4. If not cautioned, the police or prosecutor may decide to charge her with theft. The Crown Prosecution Service will apply the Code for Crown Prosecutors in deciding whether to proceed with the prosecution.

5. They will apply the evidential sufficiency test first. If there is insufficient evidence against her—for instance, no eyewitness or security camera evidence and she was not caught red-handed—they may decide not to prosecute.

6. If that test is satisfied, however, they will go on to apply the public interest test. For example, if she is found to be terminally ill or if she is very old and also senile, or has severe learning difficulties, they may decide that the public interest factors against a prosecution outweigh the factors in favour.

7. If the CPS declines to prosecute, the store may prosecute her or take a civil action against her, which would be much easier to prove, because of the lower degree of proof.

8. If prosecuted, she is highly unlikely to be remanded.

9. She will be summoned to appear in the magistrates' court as soon as possible.

10. If she is 10–17, she will appear before the youth court, a closed court, comprising mixed-gender lay magistrates or a DJMC. She will not be given the choice of a jury trial in the Crown Court and the magistrates will not send her to trial in the Crown Court, unless charged with an adult, because the alleged crime is not sufficiently grave. The press may attend the youth court and report but may not identify her. Her parents/guardians will be strongly encouraged to accompany her and the magistrates will strongly encourage her to take legal advice from the duty solicitor, if she is not already accompanied by a solicitor. If she pleads guilty, the bench may sentence her there and then, or request a report. If she pleads not guilty, there will be a trial, usually adjourned until a later date. If the bench are not satisfied of guilt beyond reasonable doubt, they must acquit her. If they find the case proven, they will convict her. They may sentence her immediately if convicted, or require a report on her by a social worker, before sentencing. Under certain circumstances, the bench may impose a referral order, in

which case she will be referred to the local Youth Offending Panel.

11. If she is an adult, she will appear before the next magistrates' court and the magistrates will take her plea before determining mode of trial. She may be advised and/or represented by the duty solicitor or a privately paid for barrister or solicitor. She may qualify for publicly funded representation under the CDS if she satisfies the means test and the interests of justice test. She will satisfy the interests of justice test if, for example, she is in danger of losing liberty or livelihood, if convicted, or if she needs an interpreter, or if she lacks full mental capacity or is in some other way vulnerable. If she is granted publicly funded help, she may be required to make contributions towards the cost. The magistrates will take account of her plea and criminal record and the allocation guidelines in determining whether to accept jurisdiction or send her up to the Crown Court for trial. They are highly unlikely to do so, whatever her plea. In this case, the choice of court then falls to her and she can ask the magistrates for an advance indication of sentence in aiding her choice but they do not have to give one.

12. If she is an adult, pleading guilty, the DJMC or magistrates may sentence her immediately, after a brief plea in mitigation, or they may adjourn for a pre-sentence report or medical or psychiatric report, if necessary.

13. If she pleads not guilty and is content to be tried by the magistrates, a bench of three or a DJMC, advised by a legal adviser, will try her later, in an adjourned hearing, to give prosecution and defence time to prepare the case. The bench will decide on guilty and innocence then and, with the advice of their legal adviser, will sentence her.

14. If she pleads not guilty and opts to be tried at the Crown Court, she is likely to be bailed to appear at a later date, while the case is transferred. Her solicitor will brief a barrister to represent her, unless the solicitor has an advocacy certificate granting rights of audience in the Crown Court. As above, she may be granted publicly funded representation.

15. At the Crown Court, she may appear at a plea and case management hearing. If she changes her plea to guilty, she may be sentenced by the judge or recorder as soon as he has the benefit of a pre-sentence report. If she maintains her plea of not guilty, the judge will fix the trial date and make other arrangements for

the trial. Any further hearing, requiring her presence, may not be necessary if everything is organised by the case progression officer. (Points on case management may be expanded).

16. If she maintains her not guilty plea, the prosecutor or her defence team may enter plea negotiations. She may be offered a sentence discount in exchange for an immediate guilty plea. (This point can be expanded).

17. If, however, she maintains her not guilty plea, she will be tried by a jury of 12, who will determine guilt or innocence and the trial will be conducted by a circuit judge or recorder, who will control procedure, determine points of law, sum up the evidence to the jury and instruct them on law.

18. At any time pre-trial or during the trial, the judge may order or direct an acquittal on a point of law or evidential sufficiency and the prosecution may appeal to the CA against such a ruling.

19. If she is found guilty by the jury, she will be sentenced by the recorder or judge.

20. If she is found not guilty, she will be acquitted and discharged. The prosecution may appeal, with leave, to the CA on a point of law, which will not affect her acquittal, or against an unduly lenient sentence, in which case the CA may increase her sentence.

21. If she has been convicted in the magistrates' court, she has an unfettered right to appeal against sentence and/or conviction to the Crown Court, where the appeal will be heard by a recorder or judge with two lay justices. If appealing against conviction, there will be a full rehearing. If she feels the magistrates' have erred on law or exceeded their jurisdiction, she may ask them to state a case (give fuller reasons) and appeal by way of case stated to the Divisional Court of the QBD. This court may quash her conviction or uphold it or remit it to the magistrates, with a direction. If she has been acquitted by magistrates, the prosecutor may appeal by way of case stated, on the same grounds. Either party may apply to the Div Court for a judicial review of the case, if they consider there was a procedural irregularity (e.g. alleged bias), or the magistrates exceeded their jurisdiction or acted unreasonably. The losing side may, with leave, appeal to the CA on a point of law, or, with leave, "leapfrog" to the UKSC, if the case is certified as raising a point of law of general public importance.

22. If she has been convicted in the Crown Court she may seek leave to appeal to the CA against conviction and/or sentence. She is likely to be refused leave and may renew her application before

the CA in person. If the CA considers her conviction is unsafe, they will quash it. They may reduce her sentence.

23. The losing party in the CA may apply for leave to appeal to the UKSC, and leave may be granted, provided the CA or UKSC also certifies that the case raises a point of law of general public importance. If the case raises a point of EU law, any court may refer it to the ECJ for a preliminary ruling under art. 234 and the CA or UKSC must refer, if they are the last court of appeal. If the case raises a human rights point, for instance over the right of silence, she may challenge the UK before the ECtHR.

24. If she has exhausted her rights of appeal and considers she has been wrongly convicted, she or anyone acting on her behalf may petition the CCRC, who, if they are convinced of a real possibility that the sentence or conviction would not be upheld, or in exceptional circumstances, may refer her conviction to the Crown Court if she was convicted in the magistrates' court, or to the CA, if she was convicted in the Crown Court.

25. If the court allows such an appeal, she may apply for statutory compensation for her wrongful conviction.

26. In addition to the points above, mention could be made of her right of silence, bail issues, the rules on pre-trial disclosure in the Crown Court and judge's rulings on a point of law and appeals against such rulings. The point on plea negotiations could have been expanded. Mention could have been made of a possible retrial following an acquittal resulting from a hung jury.

Lawyers

....

INTRODUCTION

Unlike most legal professions, the English and Welsh one is divided into two main groups, solicitors and barristers, which were traditionally characterised by their monopolies. The Bar had a monopoly over rights of audience (rights to argue a case) in the higher courts and solicitors had a monopoly over direct contact with most clients, conveyancing (transfer) of property, litigation (preparing a civil case, pre-trial) and probate (administration of a dead person's property). These monopolies were eroded in the 1980s and '90s and the legal profession has been in a state of flux since it was the subject of scrutiny by the Royal Commission on Legal Services (RCLS)1979. The 2004 Clementi proposals to restructure the legal profession resulted in the **Legal Services Act 2007 (LSA 2007).**

This chapter examines the following topics.

- Organisation and regulatory structure.
- Numbers of barristers and solicitors and diversity issues.
- Legal education.
- The dismantling of monopolies and restrictive practices.
- The Clementi Report and the resultant **Legal Services Act 2007**.
- Arguments for and against fusion.

....

LEGAL SERVICES ACT 2007

It created a new regulatory structure, the objects of which are:

- protecting and promoting public interest;
- supporting the rule of law;
- improving access to justice;
- protecting consumer interests;
- promoting competition in legal services;

- encouraging an independent, strong, diverse and effective legal profession;
- increasing public understanding of citizens' rights and duties; and
- promoting professional principles.

All the representative and regulatory bodies described below are under a duty to promote these objects.

The Legal Services Board (LSB)

This was created by the 2007 Act to oversee the eight bodies regulating different types of lawyer, including solicitors.

SOLICITORS

Structure, organisation and regulation

In 2008, there were 139,666 solicitors on the Roll, 112,433 of whom had practising certificates, in private practice, and the remainder of whom worked in commerce or the public sector. The Law Society's *Annual Statistical Reports* are on its website.

The Law Society

This is the trade union of solicitors, to "help, protect and promote solicitors across England and Wales" (website). It used to be the professional regulatory body but lost this function under the **2007 Act**.

The Solicitors Regulation Authority (SRA)

This is professional governing body of solicitors, regulating their training, discipline and standards of professional conduct. It can fine individuals and fine law firms up to £2,000 and/or apply conditions to their authorisation and refer them to the Solicitors Disciplinary Tribunal, which can levy unlimited fines on firms and their members. Appeal lies to the High Court.

The Legal Complaints Service

This impartial body handles complaints, after the function was removed from the Law Society by the **2007 ACT**. A new Office for Legal Complaints was provided for by the **2007 Act**. It may start by 2010.

Gender balance

In 2008, women accounted for 44.4 per cent of solicitors with practising certificates, representing a growth of 96.2 per cent since 1998. Almost 60 per cent of newly admitted solicitors were women. Women do not progress as readily as men. Of solicitors in private practice in 2008, 49.9 per cent of men were partners but only 22 per cent of women were. The Law Society exposed a 32 per cent median pay gap in 2008. More optimistically, McGonnell demonstrates how the regulatory objectives of the **2007 Act**, listed above, may be used to benefit women and minority solicitors. She quotes the 2009–10 business plan of the LSB to "promote equality". She cites examples of powerful clients successfully demanding that their legal providers have a certain percentage of women partners. Under the LSA, performance targets may be set and, theoretically, these could include the promotion of flexible working: (2009) 159 N.L.J. 863.

Ethnicity and social diversity

The RCLS 1979 found discrimination. It deprecated the formation of minority firms of solicitors and barristers' chambers (offices). In 1986, the Law Society belatedly established an ethnic monitoring scheme and a Race Relations Committee. The 2008 statistics show that 47 per cent of minority solicitors are concentrated in very small firms. In 2008, 10 per cent of solicitors were from ethnic minorities. 28.6 per cent of students enrolling with the Law Society were from ethnic minorities but the biggest problem they face lies in entering the profession and progressing to partnerships within it. In 2003 the Society launched a Diversity Access Scheme. See now *The Law Society Group Equality and Diversity Framework 2009–11*. In 2005, the Department for Constitutional Affairs (DCA) published a report, *Diversity in Legal Services*. It asked the top 100 law firms and top 30 barristers' chambers to publish their diversity policies by March 2006 but few did. In 2006, the Government started a campaign to encourage more people from diverse backgrounds to think of entering a legal career.

In 2008, the Ministry of Justice announced a project called *Barriers leading into law*. Thirty two aspiring students will be given sponsors or "life coaches". In 2009, the Cabinet Office published *Unleashing Aspiration*, which disclosed that half of professional occupations are dominated by those from public schools, who represent only seven per cent of the population. There is less social mobility now than post-war. It is extremely expensive to qualify as a barrister or solicitor (up to £11,000+ for the professional course and you have to support yourself) and many fail to find a job. In 2008–9, 7,000 people completed the LPC but there were only 6,000 training contracts available. Unless the excess 1,000 find contracts, they will not qualify as a solicitor. Because of the recession, some law firms offered 2008–09 trainees £10,000 to take a sabbatical.

BARRISTERS

Structure and organisation

In December 2008 there were 12,136 self-employed barristers, distributed between 690 sets of chambers, of which 342 were in London. 351 worked as sole practitioners. There were over 3,046 employed barristers. The Bar has grown considerably since 1960, when there were only 1,919 practising barristers. Statistics are on the Bar Council website.

The Bar Council

The General Council of the Bar represents the interests of barristers. It was their professional governing body but lost that function to the Bar Standards Board in advance of the **LSA 2007**. The six court circuits have their own Bar Associations, as do specialist barristers.

The Inns of Court

Each barrister must belong to an Inn of Court: Gray's Inn, Lincoln's Inn, Inner Temple or Middle Temple. Historically, they had a collegiate function. They educated students in the common law, practised in the courts, because the universities only taught civil (Roman) law. They own much of the property in which London barristers rent chambers.

The Bar Standards Board

This was created in 2006, anticipating the **LSA 2007**, taking over enforcement of professional standards and enforcing the Bar's Code of Conduct. It also handles complaints and is subject to oversight by the LSB, above.

Professional Liability

In 2000 in *Arthur JS Hall (a firm) v Simons* [2002] 1 A.C. 615 the House of Lords held that barristers and other advocates (including solicitors) could be sued for negligence in their conduct of civil and criminal proceedings. This reversed the old rule in *Rondel v Worsley* [1969] 1 A.C. 191.

The Bar's archaic practising arrangements
Chambers

Until 1990, every practising barrister had to rent a "tenancy" (really a sub-tenancy) in a "set" of "chambers" (meaning offices—note the archaic language) and until the 1980s most London chambers had to be within the Inns of Court.

The growth of the Bar led to derestriction. Barristers of three years' call may now practise independently. Securing a tenancy in a "set" of chambers is very difficult. Under the **LSA 2007**, barristers may join legal disciplinary practices, explained below, but research shows that most will not do so.

The clerk

Most "sets" have one chief clerk, or practice manager, and several juniors. All barristers must obtain their work and negotiate fees via the clerk. Historically, it was thought unseemly for barristers to negotiate fees, hence the pocket on the back of the gown, to receive the solicitor's *honorarium*, "gift for services rendered". Barristers may now sue for fees but seldom do so.

The hierarchy

The top ten per cent or so of barristers are called Queen's Counsel, more commonly called "silks", as they are entitled to wear a silk gown instead of the ordinary stuff gown. All other barristers, however elderly, are known as "junior barristers". Q.C.s take the most serious cases, charging high fees. They are appointed by the Crown. They used to be selected by the Lord Chancellor (L.C.) but, following criticism that the system was discriminatory and anti-competitive, (see below), the annual "silk" competition from 2005–06 is now organised by a company run by the Law Society and the Bar. Most juniors apply because they have built up a workload and reputation that justifies hiving off some of their preparatory work to another junior. There used to be a rule called the Two Counsel Rule whereby each Q.C. had to pay a junior to appear with them in court. This restrictive practice was abolished in 1977 but it is still widely followed. It has been the subject of repeated scrutiny and in 2000 the L.C. further restricted the use of silk or more than one advocate, in publicly funded Crown Court cases. Solicitor advocates may be appointed as Q.C.s but solicitors continue to complain about the Q.C. system and want it abolished. See below.

Partnerships

Barristers stand or fall by their own individual skills (and health). They are not allowed to form partnerships except if practising overseas but this rule will have to change because of the new business structures permitted by the **LSA 2007**. In November 2009, the Bar Standards Board decided that barristers could form barrister-only partnerships.

Pupillage

Barristers are qualified as soon as they are "called to the Bar", on passing the Bar Finals but, if they wish to practise, they must do a one-year pupillage. They accompany their "pupil-master" barrister, or work in another "approved legal environment". They can earn fees by taking cases on their own account in their second six months but having to support themselves in their first six was one of the factors which made going to the Bar so expensive. The Bar therefore provided for pupillage funding from 2002. (Pupils must be paid a minimum salary of around £10,000 p.a.)

Rules of etiquette and unwritten rules

These seem designed to mark out the Bar as an elite, relative to solicitors and clients, and many members of the public wrongly assume that barristers are more highly qualified than solicitors (who continually complain of the arrogance of barristers). They also serve as a good tourist attraction. These are some of the best known:

- Barristers wear 18th century, male, horse-hair wigs in the Crown Court and some of the senior courts. Solicitor advocates were only allowed to wear wigs from 2008.
- They sometimes use grovelling language to the bench, e.g. "may it please your Lordship". Fellow barristers were referred to as "my learned friend", whereas solicitors were simply "my friend".
- There are strict rules of dress which require all to wear dark suits. Many men wear a waistcoated suit and, under the wig and gown, this can be too hot in summer.
- In the courtroom, "silks" occupy the front row, nearest the judge, with junior barristers behind them and solicitors behind them. In the oldest courtrooms in the Royal Courts of Justice, look out for the gate which separates the silks from those behind them.
- The judicial hierarchy reflects lawyers' hierarchy. Most senior judges were Q.C.s. Most district judges are solicitors.

Gender

The RCLS 1979 found that over 90 sets of chambers contained no women and some were prepared to admit to a "no women" policy. Astonishingly, gender and race discrimination at the Bar were not outlawed until the passage of the **Courts and Legal Services Act 1990**, s.64 and, by the late 1990s, there were still sets of chambers with few or no women, or minorities. The proportion of women as practising barristers is increasing (31 and 46 per cent of self-employed and employed barristers, respectively, in 2008).

Ethnicity and Social Diversity

Black barristers complained that racism was institutionalised at the Bar. The RCLS 1979 deprecated "ghetto" chambers and ten years later, a 1989 survey showed that half of all chambers had no ethnic minorities and 53 per cent of non-white barristers were concentrated in 16 sets of chambers. The Bar established a Race Relations Committee in 1983 and an equal opportunities policy in 1991. In 2007, the Bar published a report by Lord Neuberger, *Entry to the Bar*. He wanted to attract able people from state schools. The Bar introduced a package, including a placement programme for state school children to learn about the Bar and the courts. For an evaluation of all types of discrimination pre-2000, in the two sides of the profession, see P. Thomas, *Discriminating Lawyers* (Cavendish, 2000). Cherie Booth Q.C. has repeatedly complained that commencing at the Bar is too expensive for many students (fees plus supporting yourself) and it is much more difficult to get into practice than it is for a solicitor. There are about ten times as many solicitors as barristers and, at the moment, Bar entrants have top class degrees, because chambers can afford to be so demanding.

LEGAL EXECUTIVES

Much of the everyday work of solicitors' offices is performed by legal executives. These are paralegals with specialist qualifications. The Institute of Legal Executives (ILEX) is their representative body for 24,000 legal executives and trainees. They can become partners in a legal disciplinary practice and can gain advocacy rights and can now become district judges. The ILEX website provides a description of their work and qualification process. The ILEX Professional Standards Board is overseen by the LSB.

LEGAL EDUCATION

Barristers

All-graduate entry. Non-law graduates and mature students do a one-year Common Professional Examination (CPE) or diploma in law (the academic stage), then they and law graduates take a one-year Bar Vocational Course. Students must dine 12 times at their Inn of Court. After this, successful candidates may be called to the Bar. All barristers offering legal services must undertake one year of pupillage. All must undertake continuing education.

Solicitors

Non-law graduates and mature students do the CPE or diploma in law. Then they and law graduates take the Legal Practice Course (one year). This will be more flexible from 2009–10. It will be split into two parts and may be taken in two stages, with different providers. Alternatively, they may take a four-year qualifying degree. All must complete a two-year training contract before being admitted. All solicitors must undertake continuing education.

THE GRADUAL ABOLITION OF LAWYERS' MONOPOLIES AND RESTRICTIVE PRACTICES

The Solicitors' Conveyancing Monopoly

Solicitors' best-known monopoly was conveyancing. It used to be a substantial fee-earner and the public complained of overcharging. Solicitors claimed the monopoly protected the public from charlatans. The RCLS 1979 supported the monopoly but the Thatcher Government opposed all monopolies as anti-competitive. In 1984, the Farrand Committee recommended a system of licensed conveyancers, effected by the Administration of Justice Act 1985. In 1989, Lord Mackay L.C. proposed to permit conveyancing by banks and building societies. Solicitors said there would be a danger of conflicts of interest in "one-stop shopping" by house buyers obtaining their new home, conveyancing and mortgage under one roof. They argued that the "unfair competition" from banks and building societies would extinguish most firms of high street solicitors, thus denying the public easy access to legal services. Despite this, he promoted the **CLSA 1990**.

> **KEY POINT**
>
> The statutory objective of the **Courts and Legal Services Act 1990** is "making provision for new or better ways of providing such services [advocacy, litigation, probate and Conveyancing] and a wider choice of persons providing them, while maintaining the proper and efficient administration of justice" (s.17).

The Act established a board with the general duty to develop competition in conveyancing services and to authorise practitioners. It permitted conveyancing by banks and building societies but this was so controversial it was never implemented.

Repercussions

1. The Law Society permitted solicitors to advertise.
2. Conveyancing costs fell.
3. Solicitors began selling houses.
4. The Law Society worked to identify new markets, for instance, financial services.

Abolition of the probate and litigation monopolies
The **CLSA 1990** opened up probate services to approved banks, building societies, insurance companies and legal executives but this restriction was only relaxed *very* slowly. In 2009, barristers and conveyancers were permitted to conduct probate work.

Abolishing the Bar's monopoly over rights of audience
In 1984, retaliating over the threat to its conveyancing monopoly, the Law Society re-launched an attack on the Bar's monopoly over rights of audience in all higher courts. Solicitors have always had a right to argue cases in magistrates' courts, county courts and, since the 1970s, in a very few Crown Court centres. Barristers enjoyed a customary monopoly, fixed by a committee of judges, over rights of audience in the senior courts. The RCLS 1979 rejected solicitors' arguments on the following grounds.

- If solicitors were permitted rights of audience in the Crown Court, this would destroy the livelihood of junior barristers.
- Jury advocacy involves special skills maintained with practice, which most solicitors could not spare the time to keep up.
- Since it was up to the solicitor to select a barrister, he could make a more informed selection than the client.

In 1986, the two sides established the Marre Committee to stop the battle between them. In 1988, Lady Marre recommended that solicitors should have Crown Court audience rights.

Changes made by the Conservative Government
Lord Mackay L.C. was keen to extend the Thatcherite approach to monopolies to the Bar's work. A 1989 white paper said the Government's view was that the best access to legal services was achieved by giving clients the widest choice within a free and efficient market. Amid ferocious opposition by the Bar and the judges, the proposals were enacted in the **CLSA 1990**. It provided that rights to appear could only be granted by the "appropriate authorised body" and made similar provision for the right to conduct litigation. Barristers' and solicitors' audience rights were preserved.

Repercussions
As with solicitors, the threat of having to compete for work in an open market had an important impact on the Bar. It relaxed a number of its practice rules and even had to acquaint itself with twenty-first century business practices and marketing.

- Since 1991, sets of chambers advertise and use P.R. consultants.
- The Bar promoted new areas of work and merged chambers.

- They permitted the establishment of London chambers outside the Temple.
- They allowed direct access to non-practising, employed barristers by their employers' clients.
- Direct client access has now been extended.
- They paid pupils and reformed training.
- They developed Bar Mark, a kitemarking system based on best practice.

KEY POINT

LIFE AFTER THE COURTS AND LEGAL SERVICES ACT 1990

By 2010, nothing much has happened. Licensed conveyancers did not destroy the solicitors' side of the profession, as solicitors feared it would, because, by 2010, there are under 1,100 of them and over 140,000 solicitors.

There have been arguments involving solicitors, the Bar, the judiciary and the Crown Prosecution Service (CSP) over rights of audience, since the 1970s. The Law Society can now authorise private practitioners as higher court advocates but by 2010, there are about 1,200, many of whom do not use their rights of audience. This is hardly likely to destroy the Bar of over 15,000 and the Bar continues to grow.

A frustrated Labour Lord Chancellor, the Access to Justice Act 1999 and rights of audience

The Labour L.C., Lord Irvine, signalled his impatience with the lack of progress made by the **CLSA 1990**, in opening up rights of audience beyond the independent Bar, by promoting the **Access to Justice Act 1999**.

- **Section 36** gives all barristers rights of audience in all courts and all solicitors rights of audience and rights to conduct litigation in all courts, subject only to rules prescribed by the Law Society.
- **Section 37** prohibits restrictions on rights of audience for employed lawyers. This was a great victory for the CPS, who may now send employed lawyers to appear in the Crown Court, and for employed solicitors. In a consultation paper, Lord Irvine had complained of the "sorry saga" of their six-year attempt to get audience rights. The Bar strongly opposed this on the ground that the interests of justice are better served by an independent advocate.
- **Section 39** makes audience rights portable from one profession to another so a barrister no longer loses higher court audience rights by becoming a solicitor.
- **Section 40** empowers the Bar Council and ILEX as authorised bodies to grant their members rights to conduct litigation.

- **Section 42** imposes on all advocates and litigators a duty to the court and a duty to act in the interests of justice, formerly common law duties.

The Office of Fair Trading continued to attack restrictive practices

Nevertheless, progress in opening up competition in legal services had been far too slow, according to the OFT. In its 2001 Report, *Competition in Professions*, it recommended removing unjustified restrictions on competition.

- The Q.C. system should be abolished. They questioned the system as a quality mark, and its value to consumers.
- Multi-disciplinary partnerships of lawyers and others should be permitted.
- The Bar should abolish its prohibition on direct access by most clients. This "requires customers to employ two types of lawyer".
- Advertising should be de-restricted.
- Law Society fee guidance should be abolished, as it inhibited price competition.
- Banks and building societies should be permitted to do conveyancing

The Bar responded by changing its rules, from 2003, to permit barristers of three years' call who have undertaken a special course to give legal advice, draft documents and act as advocates in certain circumstances without the intervention of a solicitor. See Heppinstall (2005) 155 N.L.J. 1360. Barristers are not permitted to litigate. In 2002, the restriction on advertising barristers' fees was removed but they cannot advertise their success rates.

The OFT was still critical

In 2002, in a response to government consultation, the OFT insisted that:

- the Q.C. system was anti-competitive, lacked quality control and was of little use to customers;
- the selection system hindered competition because the earning power and competitive position of barristers was enhanced but little extra value was offered to clients; and
- the title Q.C. was not removed from a barrister if standards dropped.

The Bar Council rejected this but in its 2003 Annual Report, the Commission for Judicial Appointments concluded that the expense of the Q.C. selection procedure was unsustainable:

"we have built up a picture of wider systemic bias in the way that the judiciary and the legal profession operate that affects the position of women, ethnic minority candidates and solicitors in relation to Silk and judicial appointments".

Q.C. system at last reformed

In 2003, the newly created Department for Constitutional Affairs (formerly the L.C.D.) published a consultation paper, *Constitutional Reform: The Future of Queen's Counsel*. It pointed out that no other profession had such an equivalent rank. Elites in other professions were recognised only by reputation, or passing examinations. To solicitors' disappointment, the L.C. announced that the Q.C. system would stay, under a reformed selection system, devised by the Bar and Law Society. Since 2006, selection is made against an agreed set of competences, using self-assessment, multiple references and an interview. Solicitors continue to complain. In a 2008 Law Society survey, over half the respondents considered that the Q.C. rank "should become a broader mark of excellence among lawyers" but a commissioned report by Sir Duncan Nicol, in 2009, advised against this, saying the 2006 system was too new to judge.

THE CLEMENTI REPORT ON RESTRUCTURING THE LEGAL PROFESSIONS AND THE LEGAL SERVICES ACT 2007 ("TESCO LAW")

Regulating Lawyers

In 2003, Lord Falconer L.C. announced another review of legal services, to be carried out by Sir David Clementi, to examine what form of regulation would best promote competition and innovation, serve consumer interests and be more accountable. He also proposed allowing banks, building societies and insurance companies to handle the financial affairs of the bereaved (probate), and permitting supermarkets and other retailers to provide legal services (thus implementing the **CLSA 1990**) and allowing law firms to use outside investment.

KEY POINT

Clementi reported in *Review of the Regulatory Framework for Legal Services in England and Wales* (2004), favouring "a regulatory framework which permits a high degree of choice" for consumer and lawyer.

- He recommended that legal disciplinary practices (LDPs) should be considered. These are now permitted by the **LSA 2007**, from March 2009. Any lawyers can be allowed to practise together. For example, legal executives can now become partners and solicitors can be managers of a firm of licensed conveyancers. A firm of solicitors can be joined by patent and trade mark attorneys. Managers can include non-lawyers. Seventy-five per cent of managers must be lawyers. LDPs can take the form of partnerships, companies or LLPs—limited liability partnerships. Individual lawyers will be regulated by their own professions. A solicitors' firm can now combine with a set of barristers' chambers (so long as the Bar Standards Board changes its rules).

- Clementi recommended investment in LDPs could come from outside owners (e.g. Tesco) but they would need to be "fit to own", and there should be no conflict of interest. An insurance company could not own, say, a personal injury firm.
- The Act permits these "alternative business structures". They may be introduced from 2011.
- Clementi also recommended reconsidering multi-disciplinary partnerships. These had been considered since the 1970s. In an MDP, solicitors could be partners with other business people, such as estate agents and accountants. The Act permits them as a type of ABS. See point above.

IMPACT OF THE LSA 2007 ON LAWYERS' BUSINESS STRUCTURES

According to Legal Risk, only five per cent of the top 100 law firms believe the Act will have "a significant" impact on them. McGonnell considers that firms that practise internationally are not likely to transform into ABS or accept outside ownership, because both are banned by the American Bar Association and there are similar problems in Europe, for instance in Germany. High Street firms will be affected because supermarkets etc. will sell commoditised, standardised legal products: (2009) 159 N.L.J. 1069. A survey by Intendance Research found almost half of lawyers surveyed thought high street firms would be drastically affected. Ironically, Tesco is not interested in the legal services market: E. Fennell, *Times*, May 21, 2009.

CLEMENTI ON COMPLAINTS

The RCLS 1979 condemned the Law Society's handling of complaints and, despite reform, it had been criticised ever since. In the **Access to Justice Act 1999**, the Lord Chancellor was empowered to appoint a Legal Services Commissioner if the Law Society did not correct the problem. In 2000 the Director General of Fair Trading gave the Law Society a "final warning" to put their house in order. In 2006, they were fined £250,000 for failing to plan how to deal with complaints adequately. There had never been criticism of the Bar Council's handling of complaints. Clementi was asked to examine complaints handling. He suggested abolishing the legal profession's right to self-regulation. There should be a new regulator, a Legal Services Board, chaired by a non-lawyer and accountable to Parliament. Its objectives would include upholding the rule of law, promoting access to justice and competition, and protecting consumer interests. It would normally delegate regulation to the professional bodies. The Bar and Law Society would have to separate their regulatory and trade union functions. All complaints would be made to an independent Office for Legal Complaints (OLC). Its aim would be to provide "quick and fair redress to consumers", including mediation and making binding orders. Discipline would be left to the Solicitors' Disciplinary Tribunal. All of these proposals were enacted in the **2007 Act**. It was heavily criticised by lawyers and had to be modified in its passage through Parliament. Critics argued that the power of the Legal Services Board would breach the UN Basic Principles on the Role of Lawyers. See (2006) 156 N.L.J. 1113. The OLC will probably be operative from late 2010.

FUSION

It has long been argued that the public would be better served by a fused profession.

Arguments for fusion

*   If a case goes to court, the client is often paying for two lawyers, a barrister and solicitor, or three if a Q.C. is employed ("three taxi meters", as Zander famously said, in *Lawyers and the Public Interest*, 1968).
*   Because the client tells the story to the solicitor, then the solicitor briefs the barrister, there may be a failure in communication and the system is inefficient.
*   Returned briefs: clients and solicitors are frequently denied their first choice of barrister, because she is unavailable, so the brief is passed to someone else in the same chambers.

Arguments against

*   Barristers can concentrate on preparing for trial, or preparing a specialist opinion, free from interruptions to meet clients.

- Jury advocacy and oral advocacy are specialist skills which need constant development.
- Loss of choice: if the profession were fused, the best barristers would join law firms and cease to be available to all clients.
- The present system is more cost effective. It is cheaper for a solicitor to brief a barrister as an advocate, because solicitors' practices have a lot of overheads.
- English procedure requires continuous hearings and solicitors cannot spare the time for this.
- Judges are not expected to research cases so they depend on the specialist legal knowledge of barristers.

Revision Checklist

You should now know and understand the following:

- the statistical distribution of barristers and solicitors and issues of diversity;

- the partial destruction of lawyers' monopolies and restrictive practices; and the reasoning behind this (to open up competition);

- the structure, education and organisation of the legal profession;

- the new regulatory structure established by the LSA 2007, including complaints handling, and background; and

- new business structures permitted by the LSA 2007 and likely impact.

FURTHER READING/UPDATING

Darbyshire on the ELS, 2008, Chapter 13
New Law Journal
The Law Society's *Gazette*

websites
Bar Council
ILEX
Law Society
Regulatory bodies, as mentioned in the text

QUESTION AND ANSWER

The Question

Explain and account for the dismantling of the monopolies and restrictive practices that separated the two sides of the legal profession and marked them out from other lawyers such as legal executives. Would a fused profession better serve the public interest?

Advice and the Answer

Advice

"Explain and account for" means tell the story of events and explain the reasons why it happened. There are two parts to the question and they are not divided into a. and b. so they may well be related. Indeed, here they are related. If all monopolies and restrictive practices are abolished then any lawyer can do anything, even if they have to acquire special qualifications, so this could ultimately lead to a fused profession, something the Bar have long feared as threatening its survival as a separate profession.

Answer guide

1. Examine the whittling away of barristers' rights of audience, solicitors' conveyancing monopoly, solicitors' monopoly over direct access to the client and their monopoly over probate services. Examine changes to the Q.C. system.
2. It does not matter whether you tell the story about monopolies in chronological order or describe what happened to the monopolies one by one, provided that there is a clear plan and you demonstrate an understanding of how the issues are related.
3. In this part of your answer, there is no need to refer to lawyers' regulatory structure.
4. Explain that this anti-monopoly policy was meant to open up competition and thus enhance consumer interests.
5. Comment on what has been achieved for the profession and the consumer.
6. Note that it has taken a long time and several Lord Chancellors to partly dismantle these monopolies and
7. we are still only part way there, because solicitors still strongly object to the Q.C. system and continue to call for its abolition.

8. Consider the pros and cons of a unified profession.

9. Acknowledge the Bar's fear that dismantling monopolies then establishing new business structures open to all types of lawyer, under the **LSA 2007** may result in a fused profession and destroy the independent Bar.

10. Though they have been expressing this fear since the 1970s, the Bar is still thriving and neither side of the profession has suffered. Indeed, examining the statistics, both sides continue to grow, year on year.

11. Reach a brief conclusion, summarizing what you have said.

Judges

INTRODUCTION

After examining judicial independence, this chapter looks at how judges are selected, appointed, trained, disciplined and removed. It examines the controversy surrounding judicial selection and composition and the slow road to reform, culminating in the **Constitutional Reform Act 2005**.

> **KEY POINT**
>
> Since the 1950s, the most controversial point about judges has been their narrow social and educational background. Indeed, it is said and is still generally true that around 75 per cent of senior judges were independently schooled, the majority being Oxbridge graduates and almost all appointed from the senior (Q.C.) rank of the Bar. Minorities and women are underrepresented. The narrowness of the judiciary was partly attributable to the old-boy network selection system, based on "consultations" with existing judges, which was not fully removed until 2006, by the **Constitutional Reform Act 2005**. The Act dismantled the tripartite role of the Lord Chancellor (L.C.), with important jobs in all three organs of government and thus an obvious breach of the separation of powers.

TYPES OF JUDGE

The court structure diagram depicts the different types of judge and indicates the courts in which they sit. Some judges, such as tribunal judges, are not dealt with here but all types are described on the Judiciary website, which also contains current statistics, including gender and ethnicity numbers. Most criminal cases are heard by lay magistrates, described in the next chapter.

- Recorders. They are lawyers who sit at least 15 days per year, in the Crown and/or county court. Since part-time sitting is normally a requirement for a fulltime post, almost every circuit and High Court (HC) judge has sat as a recorder before applying.

- District judges (DJs) in the county court. They manage and hear *most* civil cases in England and Wales. They also hear family cases. Each has sat as a part-time, deputy district judge before applying.
- District judges (magistrates' courts) (DJMCs). They hear mainly criminal cases but also civil and family. They have an identical jurisdiction to lay magistrates, except some are authorised to hear extradition cases and they tend to be used for longer and more complex cases. Like magistrates, they are arbiters of fact and law so they are very powerful. In criminal cases, they determine the verdict (guilt or innocence), decide points of law and do the sentencing. Each has sat as a deputy DJMC before applying.
- Circuit judges (CJs). Most Crown Court cases are heard by them and many sit only in the Crown Court. In trials, they sit with a jury whose job it is to bring in the verdict, so the judge determines points of law, conducts the trial, determines the admissibility of evidence and does the sentencing. Some also sit, or sit exclusively, in the County Court, hearing the more complex civil and family cases. Most HC cases outside London are heard by authorised ("ticketed") CJs. In rare civil jury trials, they conduct the trial and determine the points of law and the jury determines liability and damages. A very small number are authorised to sit in the Court of Appeal (Criminal Division) (CACD).
- District judges of the HC. They sit in the Principal Registry of the Family Division and their work is similar to a CJ hearing family cases.
- HC Masters. They manage most cases that come before the HC in the Royal Courts of Justice but not provincial HC cases.
- High Court judges. Most sit in the Queen's Bench Division (QBD), the busiest. Judges in the Chancery and Family Divisions are recruited from specialist lawyers. Most divide their time between The Royal Courts of Justice and the circuits, dating back to the 11th/12th century, when the monarch's judges travelled on circuit to dispense the king's justice in civil and serious criminal cases. Most appeals in the CACD are heard by QBD judges, chaired by a Lord Justice of Appeal. HC judges occasionally sit in the CA (Civil Division).
- Lords Justices of Appeal (L.J.s). Most sit in both Divisions of the CA, in the Royal Courts of Justice, determining appeals on points of law and fact and appeals against sentence. They also sit in the Divisional Court of the QBD. Many of them have management jobs, organising the CA and the HC and supervising the rest of the judiciary. They are normally recruited from the HC.
- UK Supreme Court (UKSC) Justices, most of whom were law lords until October 2009. They hear points of law of general public importance, from all over the UK in the UKSC and also sit in the Judicial Committee of the

Privy Council (JCPC), mainly determining appeals from the Commonwealth. Eight of the current 11 are from England and Wales and normally recruited from the CA.

THE HEADS OF DIVISION

The Lord Chief Justice
As a result of the **Constitutional Reform Act 2005,** he replaced the Lord Chancellor (L.C.) as head of the judiciary, in 2006. He represents judges' views to Government and Parliament. He is responsible for the welfare, training and guidance of the judiciary, using resources provided by the L.C., and for judicial deployment and allocating the courts' work. He is President of the Courts of England and Wales. He hears many important cases in the CA and can sit in any court. He chairs the Judges' Council and the Sentencing Guidelines Council. Since 2006, he is appointed by a specially convened panel of the new Judicial Appointments Commission.

The Master of the Rolls
The M.R. is the President of the CA (Civil Division) and Head of Civil Justice.

The President of the QBD
This post was created by the 2005 Act. He is also Head of Criminal Justice.

The President of the Family Division
He heads the Family Division of the HC and is Head of Family Justice.

The Chancellor of the High Court
This post, formerly Vice Chancellor, was renamed in the 2005 Act. He heads the Chancery Division.

INDEPENDENCE

It is a fundamental constitutional requirement that judges are independent, that is, beyond the influence of the executive government, apolitical, incorruptible and unbiased. Independence is also required as a United Nations basic principle and by art.6 of the **European Convention on Human Rights 1950 (ECHR).** Rules and conventions support this and are now bolstered by s.3 of the **2005 Act,** which places a duty on all ministers and those involved in the administration of justice to uphold judicial independence.

1. Security of tenure: under the **Act of Settlement 1700**, senior judges may only be removed by both Houses of Parliament.

2. Salaries: judges' salaries are fixed by a non-governmental body. They used to be relatively high, supposedly to prevent the temptation of corruption, but a HC judge is paid £172,000 per year in 2010, much less than they could expect to earn as a Q.C. (millions for the top earners).

3. Apolitical: judges are statute-barred from being M.P.s and by tradition they do not engage in party political debates. The office of L.C. fell foul of this rule and of art.6 of the **ECHR**, as he held important positions in all three organs of government and thus breached the separation of powers. He was speaker of the House of Lords (legislature), a very powerful cabinet member (executive) and was head of the judiciary and entitled to sit as a judge, as chair of the law lords. In 2003, the Government announced his position was no longer tenable and so he ceased to be speaker of the HL. Under the **CRA 2005**, he was replaced as head of the judiciary by the L.C.J. and he lost his former power to appoint or select most judges. Selection is now done by the Judicial Appointments Commission and appointment is by the Queen. The L.C. remains in the Cabinet as the minister in charge of the court system and legal services. In 2003, the Government also announced that the law lords offended against this rule, being peers in the House of Lords (legislature), with debating and voting rights, as well as being the UK's most important judges. The **CRA 2005** replaced the law lords with a UK Supreme Court, in October 2009.

4. Judges cannot be sued for remarks in court.

5. Parliamentarians should not criticise judges: this is a constitutional convention.

6. Politicians should refrain from criticising judges. This convention was apparently not understood by David Blunkett who, as Labour Home Secretary, frequently criticised judgments. Home Secretary John Reid and Minister Vera Baird forgot their duty, under the **2005 Act**, s.3, in 2006, when they copied the *Sun* newspaper, in mistakenly criticising an individual judge's sentencing (when, ironically, the judge was constrained by rules set out by John Reid's Home Office and guidelines prescribed by the Sentencing Guidelines Council).

7. The media should refrain from criticising judges: this convention seems to have fallen into disuse, as evidenced by the *Sun's* campaigns.

8. Freedom from interference with decision making.

9. The rule against bias: judges are disqualified by common law (the rules of natural justice), from dealing with cases in which they have an interest, proprietary or personal. This is now reiterated in art.6 of the **ECHR**.

10. Appointments: the appointment system must be independent of politics.

11. Regular use was made of judicial independence by appointing them to head inquiries into politically sensitive issues such as the Hutton Inquiry Report of 2004, which examined the circumstances surrounding the death of Dr David Kelly (a Government adviser at the time of the Iraq invasion in 2003).

In 2007, the Labour government was heavily criticised by the House of Lords Constitutional Affairs Committee, because they created a Ministry of Justice without consulting the judges and did not seem to understand the constitutional implications of this. Senior judges were concerned about judicial independence and safeguarding the courts budget.

NEUTRALITY

Writers such as J.A.G. Griffith in *The Politics of The Judiciary* (Fontana, 1977 and later editions) were, however, less concerned over the previously-declared political allegiance of the judiciary than over their narrow political and social class backgrounds and socialisation at the Bar, consciously or unconsciously influencing judges, especially in political cases (e.g. in administrative law and in cases involving labour relations, civil liberties, students and immigrants, etc.). Griffith and other critics traditionally argued, in the 1960s and 1970s, that judges showed a significantly "right-wing" approach, but this criticism could not be applied to modern judges, viewed by the Conservatives and New Labour as a liberal nuisance, regularly declaring government policy and legislation to be illegal and in breach of the **Human Rights Act 1998**. The concern remains that judges come from narrow social and educational backgrounds (over-representing Oxbridge) and there are too few women and minorities.

QUALIFICATIONS

The Courts and Legal Services Act 1990 reformed eligibility for appointment by basing it on rights of audience (rights to appear in court). Prior to the Act, solicitors of specified standing had been eligible for appointment up to the circuit bench and barristers eligible for all appointments. This had been a source of controversy between the two sides of the profession, solicitors arguing that making them eligible for the HC would widen the pool of able candidates, thus diversifying the judiciary. Whilst the **CLSA 1990** has made the handful of solicitors with rights of audience eligible, there was only one solicitor HC judge, as of 2009, and the Act was criticised, by the pressure group JUSTICE, in *The Judiciary in England and Wales* (1992). Practice as an advocate, it argued, did not guarantee the qualities necessary for a good judge and "the strong combative or competitive streak present in many successful advocates is out of place on the bench". As part of the current attempt to diversify the judiciary, the **Tribunals, Courts and Enforcement Act 2007** amended the qualifications for judicial posts. Instead of requiring audience rights (advocacy rights), or service as a lower-ranking judge, applicants must satisfy an "eligibility condition", meaning account may be taken of their experience as a paralegal, or academic, or patent or trade-mark agent. It permits the L.C. to extend qualification to legal executives and members of other designated bodies. From 2010, legal executives will be eligible to apply for DJ posts.

NEW APPOINTMENTS SYSTEM FROM 2006

The new Judicial Appointments Commission (JAC), created by the **CRA 2005**, selects judicial office holders. The 15 Commissioners comprise lawyers, judges, magistrates, tribunal members and members of the public. Twelve are appointed through open competition and three selected by the Judges' Council. The system for selection has been radically reformed by the Act, in response to prolonged criticism of the old system.

The first members of the new UKSC are mostly the existing law lords. Each time a member of the SC is needed, a special Selection Commission is appointed, consisting of the President and Deputy President of the SC and one member from the JACs of Scotland, Northern Ireland and England and Wales. The selected candidate's name must be passed to the L.C. for appointment by the Queen and he can only ask the Commission to reconsider in limited circumstances. "Acting judges", such as retired SC Justices, may supplement the SC Justices, in the same way that retired Lords of Appeal used to sit as law lords. The background discussion to this new system is contained in a 2003 Department of Constitutional Affairs consultation paper, *Constitutional Reform: a Supreme Court for the UK*.

When a new L.C.J. or Head of Division is needed, a special selection panel is now convened, consisting of two lay members of the JAC and two senior judges. As for other judges, when there is a vacancy, the JAC will select one candidate. That name is put forward to the L.C. and he may only reject or ask for reconsideration once, in very limited circumstances, otherwise he must appoint that person or put that name forward for appointment by the Queen. For Lords Justices (members of the CA) and above, the L.C. formally recommends the candidate to the Prime Minister for appointment by the Queen.

KEY POINT

The 2005 Act requires the JAC to encourage diversity and specifies that "selection must be solely on merit" and that appointees must be of good character. The L.C. may issue guidance but the selection procedure is for them to determine. This is the first time that selection criteria have been set out in statute. Under the old system, the L.C. used whatever criteria and method of selection he saw fit.

From 2006, the Judicial Appointments and Conduct Ombudsman investigates complaints about judicial appointment and ensures complaints about judicial conduct are properly handled.

Background: progressive reform

Under the old system, the L.C. effectively selected all judges, except that the most senior judges were selected by him and the Prime Minister. Considering that the L.C.'s role was a blatant breach of the separation of powers, it placed him in a very powerful position. This led to accusations of party political bias, such as when Margaret Thatcher chose Sir John Donaldson as Master of the Rolls, and cronyism, such as on the appointment of Sir Mark Potter as President of the Family Division by Tony Blair. The appointments system had been criticised in the 1970s by Griffith, the pressure group JUSTICE and others, and was progressively reformed from the 1980s, as described here, but this did not deal with the fundamental problem that selection was effectively made by a single man, the L.C., who occupied a controversially powerful role. Traditionally, all judges were selected by the "tap on the shoulder" method—invited to join the bench.

1960s and 70s

In 1968, Abel-Smith and Stevens, then a 1972 JUSTICE subcommittee considered that a more formal system of applications and references was inevitable. They suggested an advisory committee of lawyers, judges and laymen. By the 1970s, all posts lower than HC had to be applied for, the applicant naming three referees (usually judges).

Lord Hailsham's Era

In 1985, Lord Hailsham L.C. described his method of selecting judges and this system remained in place with little change until after 2000. He applied three principles:

- to appoint solely on merit;
- no single person's view on a candidate should be regarded as decisive; and
- candidates should not be appointed until they had proven themselves in a part-time capacity.

Senior civil servants gathered factual information from the candidate and opinions from the judiciary and senior members of the profession, who knew the candidate, in "consultations". These were kept on file, the factual information being open to the candidate's inspection.

Lord Mackay's Era

The Law Society argued that this system, with its reliance on advocacy experience and existing judges' personal recommendations to the L.C. discriminated against women, ethnic minorities and solicitors in general, regardless of Lord Mackay L.C.'s repeated assurances that he was keen to recruit more judges from these groups. In 1996–97 the Association of Women Barristers criticised the appointments system as being biased against women. In 1999, the Law Society announced a boycott of the consultation process, which they called "secret soundings".

Groups such as JUSTICE repeatedly criticised the system as based on the say-so of one person, a member of the government. This was an anachronism stemming from the days when the L.C. knew all the candidates. In 1992, they suggested a Judicial Appointments Commission, independent of the executive, with a majority of lay people, which would appoint all judges and supervise their training, career development and standards of performance. Lord Mackay resisted this suggestion but in 1993 he announced a programme of reform, introducing advertising of job descriptions and qualities needed below HC level. Competitions were introduced for all vacancies. A more structured basis for consultations with the judiciary and the profession was devised and lay people were involved as advisers.

Lord Irvine's Era

In 1997, New Labour came to power and announced plans for a Judicial Appointment Commission but Lord Irvine L.C. curiously retracted from them. In 1999, he asked Sir Leonard Peach to review the appointments process. The L.C. revealed that potential judges were continuously assessed by lawyers and judges for such qualities as humanity, courtesy and understanding of society. Peach's assessment was favourable but he was not allowed to comment on who should make appointments. He recommended the creation of a commission, purely to investigate grievances and complaints and to audit appointment processes and policies, and recommend changes. Its membership would closely resemble other countries' appointing commissions. For applicants of whom little was known, he recommended they nominate up to six consultees. Advocacy should no longer be an essential element in the selection process and Lord Irvine accepted that. Peach proposed alternative methods of assessing suitability, such as one-day assessment centres and psychometric testing. He thought more judges should be promoted from the lower ranks. The Law Society still called the system an "old boy" network and demanded an end to "secret soundings". In 2000, it published a report, *Broadening the Bench*, outlining its proposals for reform. From 2000, the pressure to reform the system increased. Lord Irvine responded by making continuous reforms to the system but would not contemplate reforming the office of L.C. to deal with its breach of separation of powers, or relinquishing to a commission his monopoly over appointments. He announced assessment centre pilots and accepted the need for wider advertising, better aptitude testing and an easier route from other judicial roles. A report by Kate Malleson and Fareda Banda, *Factors Affecting the Decision to Apply For Silk and Judicial Office* (LCD Research Report 2/2000), commissioned by his Department, had exposed widespread dissatisfaction with the selection process, especially among women, solicitors and minorities, who felt particularly disadvantaged by the consultations process and resented recruitment from the apparent elite group of barristers' chambers. Many other critics repeated the call for an appointments commission, including Lord Steyn (law lord) and the Society of Labour Lawyers.

Concern arose in 2001, over the apparent conflicts of interest in the L.C.'s position, when Lord Irvine solicited donations to Labour funds from lawyers. Conservatives said this was an abuse of his power over those lawyers who aspired to judicial appointments. He continued to reform the process, however. Judicial performance appraisal was extended from tribunals to the lay magistracy, then to deputy DJs in the late 1990s and to all part-time appointments, from 2001. Upper and lower age-limits for most judicial appointments were removed in an attempt to encourage more applications from women and minority lawyers and from 1998 HC posts were advertised and applications invited, though the L.C. reserved the right to invite lawyers to join the HC bench.

Assessment centres were piloted in 2002–03 for deputy DJs and masters of the HC. They were used instead of traditional interviews, to identify whether the approach encouraged more applications from groups currently underrepresented. Candidates have to show appropriate characteristics. The assessments include practical exercises and role-play, an interview and written examination. In 2003, they were reported to be a success and have been extended to recorder recruitment. In 2002, a working party recommended making CPS lawyers eligible for appointment, in order to widen the social composition of the bench. The CPS employs a higher percentage of ethnic minority, female and state-educated lawyers than the legal profession and judiciary as a whole. Government lawyers became eligible to sit as civil recorders and deputy DJMCs.

The Judicial Appointments Annual Report 2001–02 showed that the percentage of women appointed to judicial posts increased to 34.4 per cent. The proportion of ethnic minority appointments increased to 7.8 per cent. Nevertheless, the pressure for reform grew stronger and became irresistible by 2003. Sir Colin Campbell, First Commissioner for Judicial Appointments, suggested that although the system overall produced excellent judges, it lacked transparency and fairness. The CJA Annual Report 2003 criticised the system for appointing judges and Queen's Counsel as systemically biased against women, ethnic minorities and solicitors. It rejected the notion of a "trickle up" of women and minorities. The consultation process produced too little information to justify its cost and yielded some "narrow and inappropriate views". Also in 2003, Lady Hale became the first woman to be appointed as a law lord (now a UKSC Justice). She is heavily critical of the gender imbalance in the judiciary. In the same year, the Bar Council published a working party consultation on judicial appointments and silk. It proposed that appointments should no longer be made by the L.C. Also, and crucially, in 2003 a newly created parliamentary select committee scrutinising the Lord Chancellor's Department received witness evidence that the L.C.'s role, breaching the separation of powers, flouted the **European Convention on Human Rights**. At the same time, critics, most notably law lords Lords Steyn and Bingham, reiterated the call to separate the law lords from Parliament, preferably as a Supreme Court.

Lord Falconer's Era

The Government, surprisingly, responded to all this in June 2003 by announcing that the L.C.'s roles were to be broken up. Lord Irvine L.C. was replaced by Charlie Falconer, in the new post of Secretary of State for Constitutional Affairs and, supposedly, the last L.C. Simultaneously, the Government published a set of consultation papers on constitutional reform: the paper on Q.C.s referred to above, plus *Constitutional Reform: Reforming the Office of Lord Chancellor, Constitutional Reform: a New Supreme Court for the United Kingdom* and *Constitutional Reform: a New Way of Appointing Judges* (papers and responses are all on the archived Department of Constitutional Affairs (DCA) website). The last sought views on how an appointments commission should be constituted and what its powers should be, for instance, whether it should have a role in complaints and discipline. The paper on judicial appointments suggested three alternative types of JAC: an appointing commission, a recommending commission or a hybrid commission. The Government settled for the second option, and this was created in the 2005 Act, with procedure as described above.

Post-2006

The JAC did not make a good start in 2006. It had to re-run its first CJ competition, following criticism by judges, and new appointments were criticised for lack of diversity. Its chair, Baroness Prashar, said that if the judiciary was to diversify, the legal profession needed to make itself more diverse. One of the first acts of Gordon Brown's new cabinet was to publish yet another consultation paper on judicial appointments, suggesting a role for Parliament in conducting public hearings on candidates. It was sharply criticised by Zander and the subsequent white paper came to nothing. The Parliamentary Joint Committee on the draft Constitutional Renewal Bill concluded that it was too soon for any further substantial changes to the appointments system. In 2008, the Judicial Appointments Commission commissioned independent research to find out what attracts people to or puts them off applying to the senior judiciary, surveying 6000 members of the judiciary. Professor Dame Hazel Genn's report for the Judicial Executive Board on the attractiveness of senior judicial appointment, published in January 2009, helped identify why some lawyers are deterred from applying for high judicial office. (See Judiciary website news release 01/09 and hyperlink within it to the report). The JAC Annual Report 2008–09 claims success in enhancing diversity in that five female appointments to the HC bench were made, raising the number to 17, the biggest number ever. This remains a strikingly low number, however, given that there are 109 HC judges in 2009.

PROMOTION

There is no career judiciary. A circuit judge does not expect to be "promoted" to the HC. Most circuit and HC judges are recruited from the legal profession, not from the ranks of district judges. Career judiciaries are a common pattern elsewhere in Europe, where law graduates may choose to train for the judiciary rather than practise and can expect promotion in the same manner as the civil service. Their judges are consequently much younger than ours. In 1992, JUSTICE repeated its 1972 suggestion of a structured judicial career path and the Labour Government sought views on a career judiciary in its 2003 consultation paper.

SOCIAL BACKGROUND AND DIVERSITY

Apart from the fact that our judiciary is predominantly white and male (diversity statistics are on the judiciary's website), much research and comment has been devoted to their narrow social background. Griffith demonstrated that at least 75 per cent of most judicial samples surveyed came from upper or upper-middle class families, and attended public school and then Oxford or Cambridge. See now statistics published by the Sutton Trust. Lord Falconer L.C. considered lack of diversity an urgent problem. In 2004, he published a consultation paper, *Increasing Diversity in the Judiciary*, saying: "Society must have confidence in that the judiciary has a real understanding of the problems facing people from all sectors of society". The paper and responses are on the archived DCA website. In 2006, the DCA published a *Judicial Diversity Strategy*. It resulted from research on what deters women and minorities from applying. There is now a Minister for Judicial Diversity and in July 2006, she announced a plan to encourage more solicitors to apply to be judges. Fractional posts and job-shares have been promoted. Judges often give lectures on diversity. These are on the Judiciary website. (See also the **Tribunals, Courts and Enforcement Act 2007**, above.) Remember that the Judicial Appointments Commission has a statutory duty to promote diversity under the **2005 Act**. It has a JAC Diversity Forum, whose work is explained in the JAC Annual Report. The 2008–09 research reports mentioned above indicate that the following factors discourage potential applicants and these are outside the control of the JAC:

- the policy of requiring applicants to have served part-time (in fee paid work);
- lack of availability of salaried part-time working (this means the lack of fulltime appointments on a fractional basis (not to be confused with fee-paid work mentioned above);
- a lack of diversity among lawyers; and
- working conditions within the judiciary. (2008–09 Annual Report).

TRAINING

Judges receive very little, compared with European career judges, who have judicial colleges. The Judicial Studies Board (JSB) supervises brief initial training for new part-time judges in the lower judiciary and all the lower judiciary receive regular continuation training. New HC judges received no special training until 2003 and the senior judiciary are not provided with systematic continuation training or expected to attend, though in 2009, induction training is being devised and they have about six tea-time seminars per year in the Royal Courts of Justice. Specialist sessions for the whole judiciary have been run on major reforms such as the **Civil Procedure Rules 1998** and **Human Rights Act 1998**. Judges resisted training until the 1970s, on the ground that it undermined independence. Consequently, the JSB is run by judges and most training is delivered by judges. Under its current strategy, it plans to turn itself into a judicial college and it proposes that judges have five days' training per year. Given constraints on public finance, however, this is unlikely to happen soon.

REMOVAL

It is a corollary of judicial independence and immunity that judges, especially the senior judiciary, have an entrenched security of tenure, first established in the **Act of Settlement 1700**. Now, under the Supreme Court Act 1981 and the **CRA 2005** every senior judge "shall hold office during good behaviour, subject to a power of removal by Her Majesty, on an address presented to her by both Houses of Parliament". This procedure has only been used once, to remove an Irish Admiralty judge in 1830, for embezzlement.

The L.C. may remove an infirm judge, incapacitated from resigning, under the **Supreme Court Act 1981**, s.11. Under the **Courts Act 1971**, s.17, he may remove a circuit judge on the grounds of incapacity or misbehaviour, or failure to comply with his conditions of appointment. Judge Bruce Campbell was so removed in 1983 after his well-publicised convictions for smuggling large quantities of whisky and cigarettes. Under the **CRA 2005**, removal now needs the LCJ's consent and a recommendation from a special tribunal but most judges resign before this might arise, such as a circuit judge convicted for drink-driving in 2009.

COMPLAINTS

Under the **CRA 2005**, the L.C. and L.C.J. have joint responsibility for complaints and discipline of judges and magistrates and are assisted by the Office for Judicial Complaints. Previously, there was no formal system.

Revision Checklist

You should now know and understand:

- the main types of judge, including Heads of Division, the courts they sit in and the work they do;

- the eleven aspects of judicial independence;

- what is meant by judicial neutrality;

- how judges are recruited, selected, trained, disciplined and removed;

- the importance of the **Constitutional Reform Act 2005** in reforming the judicial appointment system and the role of LC;

- the background of complaints and reform that preceded the 2005 Act; and

- the problem of lack of diversity and the attempts to enhance diversity.

....

FURTHER READING/UPDATING

Darbyshire on the ELS, 2008, Chapter 14 and material referred to therein, and website updates.

Websites
Department of Constitutional Affairs (archived)
Judiciary
Judicial Appointments Commission, especially annual report and publications
Judicial Studies Board, including annual report
Office for Judicial Complaints

QUESTION AND ANSWER

The Question

Explain how and why the system of judicial appointments has recently been reformed. In your opinion, is there room for further improvement in recruiting and selecting judges?

Advice and the Answer

The reforms are explained in this book and in greater detail in *Darbyshire on the ELS*, 2008. The best sources for prompting you to think about how the system could be further reformed are the consultation papers on judicial appointments 2003 and judicial diversity, 2004, as above, and responses, archived on the DCA website. You may think, for instance, that the law should be changed so that judicial appointments are not confined to lawyers with relevant rights of audience or that the post-qualification periods stipulated in the law should be reduced. You might consider whether academics should be eligible for appointment as judges but if you make any suggestions make sure that you justify them.

Answer guide

1. Explain the traditional and current criticism of the judiciary, that it (especially the senior judiciary) is dominated by older, white males, a disproportionate number of whom were independently schooled and Oxbridge educated. See stats on diversity on the Judiciary website. Find Sutton Trust stats on educational background.

2. Explain how this was/is partly caused by the old system of recruitment, pre-2006, with its heavy reliance on existing judges' views (hardly surprising that judges recommended people like themselves).

3. Explain how it was partly caused by the historic statutory requirement for judges to be selected from barristers and solicitors with rights of audience, thus narrowing the pool significantly.

4. Describe the progressive pre-2006 reforms and the new scheme under the **CRA 2005** and the change of statutory qualifications for the bench in the **2007 Act** and show how they were intended to respond to previous criticisms and make the recruitment system fairer and open to a wider pool. Comment.

5. Acknowledge the new complaint that judges are still not being recruited from a diverse pool and the JAC's response that this is caused by lack of diversity in the legal profession itself. Cross check information in the chapter on the legal profession. See JAC website, annual reports and the research mentioned above.

6. Consider the 2004 paper on diversity and research on recruitment on the judiciary website. Think about and suggest further reforms that might help to diversify the judiciary and acknowledge any hurdles.

7. Make brief concluding remarks summarising what you have said.

Magistrates

INTRODUCTION

This chapter covers magistrates, who sit in the magistrates' court, hearing and sentencing the bulk of criminal cases and many family cases and who sit hearing appeals in the Crown Court, and district judges' (magistrates' courts) (DJMCs), the professional judges who share the work of the magistrates' court. The chapter distinguishes between unpaid, volunteer magistrates (lay justices), who are not usually legally qualified and who sit in twos and threes, for a minimum of 26 half-days per year, from DJMCs, formerly known as stipendiary magistrates, who are professionally qualified and normally sit alone, full-time. Both types are called magistrates and Justices of the Peace. Their jurisdiction is almost identical but, through an accident of history, the bulk of the case load in Inner London is heard by DJMCs while in Outer London and the provinces it is heard by lay justices. In this chapter we will learn about:

- lay justices' appointment and selection;
- the effort to secure a representative lay Bench, in terms of politics, race and social class;
- the training, removal and discipline of lay justices;
- district judges (magistrates' courts);
- comparing lay and professional magistrates (DJMCs) and suggestions for a mixed bench; and
- magistrates' clerks.

LAY JUSTICES

In 2009 there were around 29,270 lay justices, 14,798 of whom (50.6 per cent) were women and 92.4 per cent of whom were white (Judiciary website). About 2,000 new justices are appointed annually. They are unpaid volunteers, who may claim for loss of earnings and other expenses.

Appointment and selection
At the time of writing, 2009, transitional arrangements are in place, as the system may be reformed following the **Constitutional Reform Act 2005**. They

are appointed in the name of the Queen to the Commission of the Peace by the Lord Chancellor (L.C.), following approval by the Lord Chief Justice (L.C.J.). They are selected by local Advisory Committees, which consist mainly of magistrates. When it is ready to do so, the Judicial Appointments Commission will take on the responsibility for selecting magistrates which it was given in the 2005 Act, though there are no plans to do this at the time of writing (2010). Any adult under 65 can apply and it is not necessary to be a British citizen. Details of the conditions of appointment and qualities sought are on the DirectGov website. The L.C. ran the first national recruitment campaign for magistrates in 1999.

Politics, social background and race

Whereas the doctrine of judicial independence excludes full-time judges from party politics, this is not the case for magistrates. Many are local councillors. Indeed, L.C.s have directed Advisory Committees to strive to appoint politically-balanced Benches but 1995 statistics showed an overrepresentation of Conservatives. In 2003, Lord Falconer L.C. announced that voting patterns would no longer be used as indicators of whether a bench reflected the local community. They have been replaced by indicators of occupational, industrial and social groupings, matched against the census.

The work pattern of the lay magistrate excludes certain groups of the population and favours others. Some cannot spare the time to sit, e.g. those who travel extensively for their work, those who are establishing businesses and those whose promotion chances depend on their visible efforts at work. These groups tend to be under-represented on the Bench. For some, sitting as a magistrate would cause a financial loss (e.g. independent business persons and those who are paid by the hour). Justices' loss of earnings allowances are only sufficient to compensate the average to low-paid. Groups who can spare the time to sit are over-represented on the Bench (e.g. retired persons, teachers and lecturers, top management and housewives with older children). The over-representation of some of these groups can be exacerbated by the fact that, being readily available, they may sit more often than other magistrates. The L.C. set a maximum of 100 sittings per year.

The class imbalance of the Bench is a source of continuing concern. The Royal Commission on Justices of the Peace (1948) expressed disappointment that the professions and top management were significantly over-represented on the Bench, with a very low proportion of them waged. Research by Hood (1972) and Baldwin (1976) showed that the imbalance had worsened. It had not improved by 1990 (Henham). Auld L.J. emphasised the value of the lay magistracy in the Criminal Courts Review 2001 but commented that there was "scope for improvement, particularly in the manner of their recruitment, so as to achieve a better reflection, nationally and locally, of the community" (p.98).

Complaints have been made that there are too few minority magistrates. In 1987, the L.C. acknowledged that the percentage did not reflect the community but, despite his efforts, 1995 statistics showed no improvement. In 2001, his Department and Operation Black Vote launched the magistrates' shadowing scheme, encouraging members of minority ethnic communities to shadow lay justices, in the hope of enhancing recruitment. The evaluation report, *Judiciary For All*, was published in 2003. Lord Irvine L.C. said the scheme had been successful in challenging participants' views of magistrates and allowing magistrates to gain an understanding of minority communities. In October 2003, Lord Falconer launched a Magistrates National Recruitment Strategy to encourage younger people (over 80 per cent of magistrates are over 50), target ethnic minorities and the disabled, and cut sitting days. The Judicial Appointments Annual Report 2004–05 detailed progress, such as improving advertising, helping advisory committees target local underrepresented groups and engaging employers' groups. (See the archived Department of Constitutional Affairs website.) In 2005, a 20-year-old-Asian was appointed to the Horsham Bench, and his youth caused some controversy. In 2007–8, 1,899 new magistrates were appointed (source: Judicial and Court Statistics, Judiciary website), of whom 8.3 per cent were from an ethnic minority. In 2009, 92.4 per cent of magistrates were white (diversity statistics, Judiciary website). The Ministry of Justice website lists recruiting more young magistrates as a key diversity objective.

In 2004, the DCA published research on "Ethnic minority magistrates' experience of the role and of the court environment". It found that 70 per cent of respondents had wholly favourable initial impressions of their bench and 72 per cent had not encountered racist attitudes in fellow magistrates.

Training

The L.C. is responsible for magistrates' training and the Judicial Studies Board has taken on a "strengthened role" pursuant to the **Courts Act 2003**, following the recommendation of Auld L.J., in the Criminal Courts Review, to enhance consistency and quality. Training is generally provided locally, by the justices' clerk and magistrates' clerks, and organised according to the needs of the individual. After the initial induction training (usually a long weekend course), distance learning, prison visits and a few hours of observing court proceedings, if necessary, the justice may commence sitting, as a "winger". A mentor is appointed for each new justice and the justice will undertake about six mentored sittings in the first year. Training needs are assessed according to whether the justice has achieved prescribed competences and, when they are ready, they will be appraised. They receive consolidation training after about a year. After four or five years, they may choose to undertake chairmanship training. Justices appointed to youth and family proceedings courts must also undertake specialist training. Magistrates are offered regular continuation training and ad hoc training as the need arises, such as that provided on the **Human Rights Act 1998** and on other new statutes. They are appraised every three years. Statutory provision for magistrates' training is now provided in the **Courts Act 2003,** ss.19–21. Details of training are on the Magistrates' Association website and on the DirectGov website in a booklet entitled *Serving as a Magistrate.*

Removal, disqualification and discipline

The L.C. has power, under the **Courts Act 2003,** to remove a magistrate. Most are removed because they fail to fulfil the required 26 sittings per year. Justices have been removed for being convicted of a criminal offence, being made bankrupt, refusing to apply laws they disapproved of and personal indiscretions. On reaching 70, they are transferred to the Supplemental List. The L.C. may transfer to the Supplemental List any justice on the ground of incapacity (**Courts Act 2003**). Complaints are handled by the Office for Judicial Complaints. Disciplinary action was taken against 44 magistrates in 2007–8. The biggest group of complaints is about inappropriate behaviour or comments. (OJC annual report).

DISTRICT JUDGES (MAGISTRATES' COURTS), FORMERLY KNOWN AS STIPENDIARY MAGISTRATES

Professional magistrates have almost exactly the same powers as lay justices. They are lawyers who satisfy the judicial appointment eligibility condition on a five year basis, under the **Tribunals Courts and Enforcement Act 2007,** s.50. This means, generally, they must be a barrister or solicitor, although other groups, such as legal executives, can now qualify, because of the 2007 Act. They are appointed by the Queen, after selection by the Judicial Appointments Commission, like other full-time judges. In 2009, there were 136, supported by 167 deputies (Judiciary website). The **Access to Justice Act 1999** created a unified bench of district judges, with jurisdiction throughout England and Wales, renaming stipendiary and metropolitan stipendiary magistrates.

COMPARING LAY JUSTICES AND DISTRICT JUDGES (MAGISTRATES' COURTS) AND SUGGESTIONS FOR A MIXED BENCH

In research reported in *The Role and Appointment of Stipendiary Magistrates* (1995) Seago, Walker and Wall found that:

- very few courts had rules for allocating work to stipendiaries (now DJMCs);
- most were assigned general list cases but they also heard long, complex or highly publicised trials and had a heavier caseload than lay justices;
- they handled all types of work more speedily than lay justices; and
- one provincial stipendiary could replace 32 justices and one metropolitan stipendiary could replace 24.

They suggested work could be shifted from the Crown Court: "Consideration could be given to an enhanced jurisdiction (up to two to three years imprisonment) for a trial tribunal consisting of a stipendiary and two lay magistrates" (p.145).

In 2000, research by Morgan and Russell: *The Judiciary in Magistrates' Courts* (Home Office website) made the following findings.

- Lay justices averaged 41.4 sittings per year, plus a week on training and other duties.
- Stipendiaries' (now DJMCs') work allocation was the same as Seago et al found.
- Stipendiaries' time was concentrated on either-way rather than summary (less serious) cases.
- If their caseloads were identical, they could deal with 30 per cent more appearances than lay justices.
- Stipendiaries showed more command over proceedings and court users had more confidence in them as efficient, consistent, questioning appropriately and giving clear reasons.
- Lawyers admitted to preparing better for stipendiaries.
- Lay justices were less likely to refuse bail or use immediate custody as a sentence.
- One stipendiary could replace 30 lay justices.
- Doubling stipendiary numbers would cut down court appearances but increase the prison population.
- The net cost would be about £3 million per year.
- Few members of the public had heard there were different types of magistrate.
- Most thought lay justices would be better at representing the views of the community and sympathising with the defendants' circumstances but that stipendiaries would be better at making decisions on guilt and innocence.

In 2000–01 the Institute for Public Policy Research commissioned a MORI poll on the magistracy and then asked Andrew Sanders to compare the skills and experience which lay and professional magistrates brought to the bench. His

2001 paper, *Community Justice-Modernising the Magistracy in England and Wales* reported that:

- a third of respondents did not know the majority of magistrates were lay people and
- hugely underestimated the proportion of cases they heard.
- 42 per cent would be more confident in a mixed panel.

Sanders concluded that the skills of both professional and lay magistrates were needed in deciding complex cases: legal skills to apply the relevant law to the facts and social skills to assess character and judge honesty, as well as more practical managerial and administrative skills. Panel decision-making was preferable to sole decision-making. The Civil Liberties Trust, in its report, *Magistrates' Courts and Public Confidence-a Proposal for Fair and Effective Reform of the Magistracy* (Liberty website) also recommended mixed tribunals.

In the Criminal Courts Review 2001, Auld L.J. considered this research and the arguments in favour of lay justices or professionals. He concluded that they both did a good job in their separate ways and should retain the summary jurisdiction but should not routinely sit together. As part of his recommendation for a unified criminal court, which was never implemented, he recommended a mixed tribunal as a new middle tier, to hear either-way cases likely to receive up to a two-year sentence. The Bench would comprise two lay justices and a judge, usually a district judge, or judge alone, if the defendant so chose and the court consented. There was considerable opposition to this proposal, notably from the legal profession, as it would remove the right to jury trial in the Crown Court for a large number of either-way cases. Because of this and because of the upheaval necessitated in restructuring the criminal courts, the Government rejected the suggestion, in its 2002 White Paper, *Justice for All*. Nevertheless, it planned to shift more work down into the magistrates' court by another means. The **Criminal Justice Act 2003**, s.154 doubles the magistrates' maximum sentencing power to one year's custody for a single offence, though it has not yet been put into effect. Magistrates who were the subject of doctoral research by Herbert were opposed to this change. Many felt they were already being asked to handle cases at the extreme of their ability. See synopsis by Zander at (2003) 153 N.L.J. 689 and full report by A. Herbert, "Mode of Trial and Magistrates' Sentencing Powers" [2003] Crim. L.R. 314.

MAGISTRATES' CLERKS

Both lay justices and DJMCs are advised by magistrates' clerks. The chief clerk at each court is called the justices' clerk. A justices' clerk may be in charge of more than one Bench and the nationwide trend of the last four decades has been to amalgamate Benches under one clerkship. Whereas in the 1970s, there were hundreds of justices' clerks, in 2009, there were just 49, all professionally qualified. Justices' clerks and staff used to be selected and appointed by magistrates' courts committees but are now part of Her Majesty's Courts Service.

Of course, since justices' clerks are responsible for several courtrooms, normally at more than one court, they delegate advisory functions to assistants. The staff whose job includes advising magistrates in court are called court clerks or legal advisers, of whom there are over 1,800, and they did not need to be professionally qualified until 2010. Delegated legislation requires that, if not professionally qualified, court clerks should be law graduates or equivalent, or possess a special clerks' diploma in magisterial law, or be qualified by five years' experience before 1980. A 1995 survey of court clerks' qualifications showed that under half were professionally qualified barristers or solicitors and the Conservative Government refused to require them to be qualified. This has led to the curious situation where, in many provincial courtrooms, the court clerk advising the lay justices was not professionally qualified. More anomalous is the fact that in Inner London, where most cases are heard by district judges, most clerks have been professionally qualified for decades. In 1999, the L.C.'s Department responded to these criticisms and introduced delegated legislation requiring all clerks to be lawyers by 2010 but exempted the over-40s and those in office before 1998, meaning that there are many advisers in these groups who are not professionally qualified lawyers.

Revision Checklist

You should now know and understand:

- the significance of magistrates in the English legal system and the work of their courts;

- the difference between lay justices and district judges (magistrates' courts) and what research has shown about the differences in the way they work;

- the systems of selecting, appointing and training magistrates and the problems of securing a Bench that represents the population; and

- the role of magistrates' clerks (legal advisers).

FURTHER READING/UPDATING

Darbyshire on the English Legal System (2008), Chapter 15, material referred
to therein and website updates
Justice of the Peace; *The Magistrate*, both on *Westlaw*.

websites
DirectGov
Judiciary (statistics)
Justices' Clerks' Society
Magistrates' Association
Ministry of Justice

QUESTION AND ANSWER

The Question

Lord Chancellors have sometimes boasted that magistrates represent a
cross-section of society. To what extent is this true? Explain the attempts
that have been made to achieve this.

Advice and the answer

Advice
Do not forget that magistrates include DJMCs, as well as lay magistrates.

Answer guide
   1.   Briefly consider why Lord Chancellors often say this. This is more
        of an aspiration than a statement of truth, because magistrates
        are meant to represent lay people, judging and sentencing their
        fellow humans in the majority of criminal cases. Symbolically,
        their abstract and concrete representativeness of the population
        is very important, then. L.C.s often say "cross-section" or "repre-
        sentative" in morale-boosting speeches to the Magistrates'
        Association so look for the latest L.C.'s speech on the Ministry of
        Justice website. (The L.C. is also the Justice Minister).
   2.   Cite the statistics on magistrates on the Judiciary website and
        compare them with the adult population of England and Wales
        in the last census (Office for National Statistics is the official, free,
        government website).

3. Consider whether lay magistrates are representative of both genders. Clearly they are almost perfectly representative and much more so than professional magistrates, DJMCs, whose statistics are also on the judiciary website.

4. Do they represent the ethnic breakdown of E & W?

5. Do they represent adult age distribution in E & W? Almost certainly not, since over 80 per cent of them are over 50. Why is that and why is it undesirable?

6. Do they represent a social distribution? You cannot answer this from the official statistics but look at the points made above. Certain groups are over-represented and it is very difficult to attract other groups. Why?

7. Consider my important point above, that even if a representative lay bench could be constructed, the people who can spare more time sit more often than others. You might speak to the magistrates' clerks (legal advisers) of your local magistrates' court to ask whether some magistrates sit more than others and you can go and visit your local court frequently and see for yourself what the bench looks like. Does it appear to represent the local population, or do you expect to see a predominance of white, white-haired females?

8. Are professional DJMCs more or less representative? They are younger but, by definition, they are all middle class, because they are all lawyers.

9. Why does the L.C. want to attract a more diverse bench? Back to the legitimacy point again (1).

10. What steps has he taken to try to recruit a more balanced bench? See above and archived DCA website.

11. Consider whether it will ever be possible or desirable to recruit a cross-section of the population. People with criminal records are excluded, as are people with insufficient command of the English language. They are excluded from juries too. Look at the magistrates' selection criteria on the DirectGov website. What groups does that exclude? Most people have no idea who magistrates are or what they do, let alone that any adult can apply to be one. Can you think of other ways to attract under-represented groups? Even if every member of the adult population knew they could apply, could they be bothered to be a magistrate? Can you think of anything to attract them?

The Jury

10

INTRODUCTION

Juries mainly sit in the Crown Court where, if the defendant pleads not guilty, he has to be tried by a judge sitting with 12 jurors. The judge decides points of law, conducts the trial and does the sentencing, and the jury brings in the verdict of guilt or innocence, on the evidence. Juries are also used in coroners' courts and in the civil courts but their use is rare in the latter. This chapter examines eligibility for jury service and the arguments surrounding the jury.

ELIGIBILITY

Historically, the jury were like witnesses, local people who knew something of the defendant or alleged incident. From the nineteenth century, jury service was confined to owners of property over a certain value. Eventually, all house-holders became eligible. Later, the property qualification was abolished and jury selection was laid down in the Juries Act 1974, as amended by the **Criminal Justice Act 2003**. Those qualified are people on the electoral register, aged 18–70, who have lived in the UK for five years since the age of 13. The Act does not stipulate random selection.

The Act destroyed randomness by including long lists of the disqualified, the ineligible and the "excusable as of right". This, along with discretionary excusal by the court, destroyed randomness and was criticised by Auld L.J. in the *Criminal Courts Review*, Ch.5 (background research in Darbyshire et al, "What can the English Legal System learn from jury research published up to 2001?" accessible on Kingston University website).

KEY POINT

Auld L.J. recommended that everyone should be qualified for jury service, except the mentally ill. This was accepted by the Government and was enacted in Sch.33 to the **Criminal Justice Act 2003**. This was controversial, since doctors, nurses, lawyers, judges and criminal justice professionals may now be summoned. Only serving members of the armed forces have a *right to excusal*, if certified by their commanding officer.

He recommended that the category of the *disqualified* should not change and this was accepted by the Government. Consequently, the **2003 Act** preserves the disqualification of people on bail, people who have ever been sentenced to custody or alternatives for five years, or who, in the last 10 years, have been so sentenced.

Selection from the electoral roll
This is done randomly. The roll is problematic. It is not accurate, because of population mobility, house moves, death, and people not registering, especially to evade council tax. Auld L.J. recommended that, as in the US, the roll should be supplemented by other publicly maintained lists or directories. (For background detail, see the paper by Darbyshire et al, above). The Government rejected this recommendation.

Discretionary excusal
Section 9 (2) of the **1974 Act** permitted further inroads into randomness by allowing jury summoning officers to accept excuses for good reasons. Acceptable excuses were highly subjective.

KEY POINT

In 2000, the Jury Central Summoning Bureau (JCSB) was introduced, administering a nationwide summoning and excusal system, endeavouring to ensure consistency, following a 1999 Home Office survey by Airs and Shaw exposing widespread and inconsistent excusals.

Despite the new scheme, however, Darbyshire et al reported, in 2001, that the Bureau had found that a very large proportion of those summoned ignored their summonses and were not pursued by the court. Auld L.J. recommended prohibiting easy excusals. Consequently, the **Criminal Justice Act 2003** places a duty on the Lord Chancellor (L.C.) to issue guidelines and this was done in 2003, on Her Majesty's Courts Service website. They run the Bureau. Since 2004, only those who can prove that they cannot *defer* service are excused. Compelling reasons for deferral include a pre-booked holiday or death or illness of a close relative. Compelling reasons for *excusal* include insufficient understanding of English, certain care responsibilities and religious beliefs that are incompatible with jury service. In the press release announcing this stricter line on excusals, the Government claimed that the **2003 Act** would double the number of those eligible for jury service. As judges and lawyers can now be summoned for jury service, lawyers' professional bodies and the Lord Chief Justice (L.C.J.) have issued guidance on when they should ask for a transfer to a different court, because lawyers summoned for jury service at the Old Bailey kept being excused, destroying the purpose of the Act.

The law lords heard three test cases on these provisions of the 2003 Act. The appellants claimed the inclusion of certain jurors, police officers and a Crown Prosecution Service lawyer, prejudiced the fairness of their trials, in *R. v Abdroikov and joined cases* [2007[UKHL 37. The law lords upheld their claims of bias. Justice had not been seen to be done. Dissenting, Lord Roger said the judgment drove a coach and horses through the 2003 Act. Zander called this a "troublesome decision": (2007) 157 N.L.J. 1530. It was applied by the CA in *Khan* [2008] EWCA Crim. 531. A police officer who had been involved in drugs operations sat as a juror on a drugs trial. The Court dismissed the appeal, applying "the fair-minded observer" test: would a fair minded observer consider this may have affected the outcome of the trial? Familiarity with an offence would not lead an objective observer to suspect a police-officer juror of bias.

Excusal by the judge

Under the **Juries Act 1974**, s.10, the judge may discharge from service any juror about whom there is doubt as to "his capacity to act effectively as a juror" because of physical disability or insufficient understanding of English. Additionally, judges have a common law discretion to discharge jurors—for instance those who have any connection with the parties. People who have been denied excusal by the JCSB regularly ask judges if they can be excused, by writing letters or asking in the courtroom. There has been no research as to how judges exercise this discretion. In 2006, a new version of the **Consolidated Criminal Practice Direction** was issued (HMCS website). Guidance to judges appears at para.IV.42.1. It is very vague: "Such applications must be considered with common sense and according to the interests of justice".

Removing jurors from a jury

The group attending a particular Crown Court, from which juries are selected during a two-week period, is called "the panel" and there are a number of ways in which any one of them can be removed from a specific jury.

Vetting

Checks may be made against the names of the jurors on the panel in certain instances. The Attorney General's (A.G.'s) 1980 guidelines distinguish between (a) vetting carried out by the police and (b) "authorised checks", requiring his personal consent.

- Police may make checks against criminal records, following guidelines set down by the Association of Chief Police Officers, to establish that jurors are not disqualified.

- "Authorised checks" are very rare and take place in trials involving national security, such as terrorist trials, and those of offences under the **Official Secrets Act 1989**. They are carried out only with the A.G.'s permission, following a recommendation by the Director of Public Prosecutions. The DPP decides what part of the information disclosed should be forwarded to the prosecution (note: not the defence).
- In cases falling under the guidelines, after an "authorised check", the A.G. will consider and, in other cases the Chief Constable may consider, defence requests for information revealed on jurors.

Challenges to the array

Once the panel has been assembled, all parties have a common law right, preserved by s.12 (6) of the **Juries Act 1974**, to challenge the whole panel, on the grounds that the summoning officer is biased or has acted improperly, e.g. this was attempted in *Danvers* [1982] Crim. L.R. 680 by a black defendant, on the grounds that the all-white jury did not reflect the ethnic composition of the community.

Challenge by the prosecution

The prosecution may exclude any panel member from a particular jury by asking them to "stand by for the Crown" without reasons, until the whole panel, except for the last 12, is exhausted. Reasons ("cause"), must be given for any further challenges but, with panels often consisting of 100 or more, the prosecution rarely needs to explain its challenges. The A.G. announced, in 1988, that this prosecution right would be limited to two instances: to remove a "manifestly unsuitable" juror or one in a in a terrorist or security trial where the A.G. has authorised vetting.

Challenges by the defence

Once the jury are assembled, the defence may challenge any number for cause (good reason acceptable to the judge), but what is an acceptable "cause" was qualified by a 1973 **Practice Note** issued by the Lord Chief Justice, who stated it was contrary to established practice for jurors to be excused on grounds such as race, religion, political beliefs or occupation.

Until 1988, the defence could make a number of *peremptory* challenges, without reasons. This was abolished, amidst great controversy, by the **Criminal Justice Act 1988**. This resulted from unsupported allegations that the right was being abused by defence lawyers, and the recommendation of the *Roskill Committee on Fraud Trials* 1986 that it be abolished. This leaves a gross imbalance between prosecution and defence rights but although challenges were controversial in the 1980s, the argument has died down because they are rarely used by either side. In this respect, English and Welsh courts are the opposite of American ones.

Race

Auld L.J. considered the research paper by Darbyshire et al, which concluded that the preponderance of research, worldwide, suggested that jury verdicts were affected by the racial composition of the jury. Like the **Royal Commission on Criminal Justice 1993**, he recommended that in a case where race was relevant, a scheme should be devised for selecting up to three ethnic minority jurors. The Government rejected this, after consultation (*Justice for All*, 2002). In *R. v Smith (Lance Percival)* [2003] EWCA Crim 283, the CA affirmed that a jury may not be racially constructed.

In 2007, the Ministry of Justice published research by Thomas, *Diversity and Fairness in the Jury System*. She found "there was no significant underrepresentation of minority groups among those summoned at virtually all" Crown Courts (p.i), although some groups were underrepresented in some courts, because of inadequate command of English "Almost half of all Pakistani jurors summoned did not serve" (p.95). She also challenged many earlier findings by jury researchers and writers as "myths". See critique by Darbyshire at [2008] Crim. L.R. 888 and reply by Thomas at 891.

....

CONTROVERSIES SURROUNDING THE JURY

There is a debate between civil libertarians and others about the pros and cons of retaining the jury and jury equity.

Should the jury be retained and does it inject layman's "equity" into the legal system?
Pro

1. The jury rouses strong emotions and is defended as a "constitutional right" and a guardian of civil liberties. Devlin hailed it as a guardian of democracy, "the lamp that shows that freedom lives" (*Trial by Jury*, Hamlyn, 1956) and Blackstone called the jury "the glory of English law . . . the liberties of England cannot but subsist so long as this palladium remains sacred and inviolate" (*Commentaries on the Laws of England*, Vol. IV, 1768). It is argued that it acts as a check on officialdom, on the judge's power, and as a protector against unjust or oppressive prosecution, applying jury "equity"—deciding guilt or innocence according to a non-lawyer's feeling of justice rather than by applying law to facts proven beyond

reasonable doubt. In *R. v Wang* [2005] UKHL 9, the HL held that there were no circumstances in which a judge could direct a jury to convict, though the CA qualified this in *R. v Caley-Knowles* [2006] EWCA Crim 1611.

2. Jury trial is argued to be fairer than trial by judge alone, since it is likely that 12 people will cancel out one another's prejudices.

3. A decision by representative members of the community confers legitimacy on the verdict. People are more likely to accept it than a judge's verdict.

Con

1. The importance of the jury system is overrated. When given the choice, most defendants choose to appear before magistrates (source: annual *Criminal Statistics*, Home Office website) and, of the remainder who opt for the Crown Court, about three-quarters plead guilty and thus are not tried by jury but just sentenced by the judge. Thanks to this and the downgrading of offences, only around one per cent of defendants are now tried by jury (Darbyshire, 1991).

2. Use of civil juries has declined since the nineteenth century. The Administration of Justice (Miscellaneous Provisions) Act 1933 imposed limits on the use of civil jury trial, which remains available only in cases of libel, slander, malicious prosecution, false imprisonment and fraud but the court can refuse it. Civil juries are rarely used. Examining the reasons why people do not opt for them gives an idea of the drawbacks of jury trial. For example, the Faulks Committee 1974 recommended jury trial should no longer be available as of right in defamation actions for these reasons.

   - Judges were not as remote from real life as popularly supposed.
   - Judges gave reasons; juries did not.
   - Juries found complex cases difficult.
   - Juries were unpredictable.
   - Juries were expensive (jury trial is more time consuming, as explanations have to be geared for them, not a judge).

3. Additional anti-jury arguments are:

   - They do not always take notes, are not encouraged to do so, and may not be able to remember all the evidence, thus they are likely to be swayed by the more dominant characters' interpretation or recollection of events. They are more likely than a judge to be distracted from deciding on the evidence by the appearance and personalities of the witnesses.
   - They have difficulty in understanding evidence in some trials. This is most acute in long and complex fraud trials, discussed below.

- The notion that the jury applies its own equity has no substance. Baldwin & McConville in *Jury Trials* (Clarendon, 1979) found no evidence that juries acquitted people in the face of unjust prosecution. On the contrary, perverse verdicts (contradicting the evidence) occurred at random. The jury thus had the disadvantage of being unpredictable. Auld L.J. considered perverse verdicts at length, in Ch.5 of the *Criminal Courts Review*, and recommended that statute should prescribe that juries had no right to acquit defendants in defiance of the law or disregard of the evidence. This provoked widespread opposition from the legal profession, politicians and other interested parties. They pointed out that the ability of a jury to apply its own equity is one of the traditional justifications for its use in determining verdicts in serious crimes. The Government rejected this recommendation.

Fraud Trials

These were considered by the Roskill Committee on Fraud Trials in 1986. Serious and complex fraud trials are notoriously long (often over 100 days), expensive and highly complicated. The Committee recommended the jury be abolished in complex criminal fraud cases and be replaced by a Fraud Trials Tribunal of a judge and two lay members with, where appropriate, a knowledge of accountancy and bookkeeping. Calls for the jury's replacement in serious frauds were renewed after the costly Maxwell brothers' trial in 1995–96. In 1998, the Home Office published a consultation paper and in 2000 the Fraud Advisory Panel suggested a number of reforms. In his *Criminal Courts Review* 2001, Auld L.J. recommended empowering trial judges, in serious and complex frauds, to order trial by judge alone or by a judge and laypeople. The Government accepted the recommendation on trial by judge alone but rejected developing a panel of laypeople. Accordingly, s.43 of the **Criminal Justice Act 2003** permitted this, under certain conditions, where the judge considered that the length and/or complexity of the trial would be unduly burdensome on jurors.

> **KEY POINT**
>
> Section 43 was very controversial and was only passed because the Government promised not to implement it without further consultation. It has not been implemented because when the Lord Chancellor tried to do so, in 2005 then 2006, it provoked strong opposition.

Nevertheless, the collapse of the London Underground Jubilee Line extension corruption trial in 2005 because of juror problems, after almost two years and a cost of £60 million, caused fresh calls for non-jury trials in these cases. The

Lord Chief Justice said that fraud trials should be reorganised so they normally took only three months and the Attorney General launched a fraud review, reporting in 2006. In 2006, the Home Secretary introduced the Fraud (Trials without a Jury) Bill, rather than activating the controversial section of the Criminal Justice Act 2003 but it was predictably defeated, in the Lords, after opposition by the Law Society, the Bar and JUSTICE. The A.G. continued to be concerned about the declining conviction rate in serious frauds and, in a change of tactic discussed in the 2008 consultation, planned to induce more guilty pleas by offering formal plea bargains.

Judge-alone trials

Because of increasing allegations of jury tampering or "nobbling", Auld L.J. recommended in his 2001 Review that a judge should be empowered to order trial by judge sitting without a jury, in such cases. This was enacted in s.44 of the 2003 Act. The prosecution can apply for a non-jury trial if there is "evidence of a real and present danger that jury tampering would take place" and that security measures would not prevent tampering. In 2009, the CA ruled that the requirements of the section were satisfied in the case of four defendants for a 2004 armed robbery. The robbery had already resulted in three trials costing £22 million. The third collapsed after a "serious attempt at jury tampering", according to the trial judge. The prosecution had applied under s.44 but Calvert-Smith J. was satisfied that the trial could go ahead, spending up to £6 million and using 82 police officers on jury protection but the CA reversed the decision and ordered a non-jury trial under s.44. See F. Gibb, "First trial without a jury for 400 years" *Times*, June 19, 2009. Remember that in the magistrates' court, many trials are conducted by a DJMC sitting alone. In the US and Canada, the accused can opt for a judge-alone trial and many defendants choose this. (For details see Auld's *Review*). He recommended that defendants in England and Wales should have the same choice. The Government tried to introduce it in the 2003 Bill but it was defeated in Parliament.

Jury secrecy

Juries deliberate in the secrecy of the jury room and disclosure of deliberations is a contempt of court under the Contempt of Court Act 1981. This ban includes research which involves questioning jurors on their decision-making. There is also a common law rule, confirmed by the House of Lords, in *Mirza* [2004] UKHL 2 that the court will not investigate or receive evidence about anything said in deliberations, applied in *Smith and Mercieca* [2005] UKHL 12. In 2005, the DCA published a consultation paper, *Jury Research and Impropriety*. This was provoked by a series of cases in which jurors had made allegations of improper behaviour by other jurors, such as racist comments, or relying on information downloaded from the internet. The paper set out the Government's view:

research should be confidential and only carried out if permitted by the minister in accordance with a code of conduct, and that the common law should be left as it is. The paper and responses are on the archived Department of Constitutional Affairs website.

Revision Checklist

You should now know and understand:

- in which courts juries sit and what their function is;

- how juries are selected;

- who is eligible for jury service;

- how and why the **Criminal Justice Act 2003** and the creation of the JCSB altered the system of summoning and excusing jurors to respond to concerns over jury composition;

- how and why jurors can be excluded from serving on particular juries; and

- the arguments raised in controversies surrounding the jury, including the pros and cons of using lay people as decision makers in this way, the debate about removing juries from serious and complex fraud trials and issues about jury secrecy and impropriety.

FURTHER READING/UPDATING

Darbyshire on the ELS (2008), Chapter 16 and material referred to therein and website updates.

Criminal Courts Review, Chapters 5 and 11, CCR website.

P. Darbyshire, A. Maughan & A. Stewart, *What Can the English Legal System Learn From Jury Research Published up to 2001?* Research for the Criminal Courts Review, Kingston University website.

C. Thomas, *Diversity and Fairness in the Jury System, Ministry of Justice Research Report 02/07* (2007), MoJ website.

Critique of Thomas by Darbyshire and response by Thomas, 2008, as referred to above, on *Westlaw*.

P. Devlin, *Trial by Jury* Hamlyn, 1956.

P. Darbyshire, "The Lamp That Shows That Freedom Lives—is it worth the candle?" [1991] Crim. L.R. 740.

Her Majesty's Courts Service website, especially information about jury service and the **Consolidated Criminal Practice Direction**.

QUESTION AND ANSWER

Outline the arguments for and against jury trial and consider recent attempts to reduce the use of jury trial.

Advice and the Answer

You need to consider both the material in this chapter and the section of the criminal procedure chapter on mode of trial, because it considers in depth the arguments about the superiority of jury trial and Crown Court trial in general, provoked by attempts to remove the defendant's right to elect jury trial in either-way cases. "Recent attempts" really include events since the recommendations of the Royal Commission on Criminal Justice 1993, not the demise of the civil jury in the twentieth century, but you might acknowledge the latter very briefly.

Answer guide

1. List and comment on the arguments in favour of jury trial, starting with Devlin and Blackstone and remembering not to underestimate the very strong attachment the English and Americans have to trial by jury for serious criminal cases, as reflected in lawyers' and politicians vociferous objections to any attempt to reduce jury trial, described in the "mode of trial" section of the chapter on criminal procedure, and expressed by judges, in cases such as *McIlkenny*, cited in the appeals section of the criminal procedure chapter.

2. In the context of the above, do not forget to mention the obvious arguments, such as safety in numbers, ordinary person's judgment on guilt an innocence, using their collective life experiences, symbolic use of lay people conferring legitimacy on the verdict, making it more acceptable to the defendant and the public, and so on.

3. List and comment on the arguments against.

4. In answering the second part, tell the story of the many recent failed attempts to remove the defendant's right to elect jury trial, told in the criminal procedure chapter.

5. Then add in the sections of the **CJA 2003** described above, permitting the judge to order trial by judge alone but remember that the

provision for judge-alone trials in serious and complex frauds was never brought into force, as it was so unpopular.

6. Remember s.13 of the **Domestic Violence, Crime and Victims Act 2004**.

7. You might like to add a brief paragraph on Auld L.J.'s suggestion that the defendant ought to be able to opt for trial by judge alone instead of jury trial. This was included in the **Criminal Justice Bill 2003** but defeated in Parliament.

8. Mention the general point that, apart from 4 to 7 above, there has been progressive reclassification of criminal offences downwards, as explained in the criminal procedure chapter, with indictable offences reclassified as either-way and either-way reclassified as summary and, very recently, fixed penalties now commonly imposed for public order offences and minor theft cases such as shoplifting. All of this has resulted in shifting more and more cases out of the Crown Court and thus out of the ambit of jury trial.

Legal Services (Legal Aid)

....
INTRODUCTION

Access to Justice

This phrase has been used repeatedly since about 1995. It encompasses access to the courts, via cheap and simple procedure, which was the intention of the Woolf Reforms (see civil procedure chapter), and being able to afford legal services, including legal advice and help with legal problems. Different types of legal aid have been developed since the mid-twentieth century and some publicly funded help was available before that. Article 6 of the **European Convention on Human Rights 1950** requires that publicly funded legal services should be available where necessary *in the interests of justice*. In this chapter we examine the following.

* Legal services (legal aid) from 2000, under the **Access to Justice Act 1999**.
* *Modernising Justice*—the policy behind the Act.
* The development of the new model, from 2000.
* More background: why was the old legal aid scheme scrapped?
* Developments since 2000 and evaluation of the current legal services scheme.
* Lord Carter's Review of legal aid procurement.

KEY POINT

HISTORY

A national, statutory scheme of legal aid and advice for civil legal problems was established by the **Legal Aid and Advice Act 1949**, resulting from the Rushcliffe Committee 1944–45. The scheme developed was the *judicare* model, the provision of services by paying fees from state funds to private practice lawyers. Rushcliffe's second suggestion, of a network of legal advice centres, staffed by fulltime state-salaried lawyers, like NHS doctors, was never implemented. Criminal legal aid was developed from the 1960s, including duty solicitor schemes in magistrates' courts and police stations. Legal advice was developed separately. The three schemes were brought together under the **Legal Aid Act 1988**, which created the Legal Aid Board. In 2007, Sir Henry Brooke, a retired appeal judge, said that most lawyers, like him, used to undertake legal aid work and the legal aid scheme used to be "the envy of the world".

LEGAL SERVICES FROM 2000

The Access to Justice Act 1999—replacing legal aid
Civil legal aid was largely replaced, in 2000, by a new *legal services* scheme, provided for in the **Access to Justice Act 1999**. Criminal legal aid was replaced by the Criminal Defence Service. Nevertheless, lawyers still refer to these services as "legal aid". The Minister of Justice (Lord Chancellor) is responsible for legal services. Lord Irvine L.C. explained his plans for these schemes, in a 1998 White Paper, *Modernising Justice*, which is on the archived DCA website. Up-to-date detail can be found in the Legal Services Commission's publications.

The Legal Services Commission

The 1999 Act replaced the Legal Aid Board with the LSC. It manages publicly funded legal services. It consists of 7–12 members, appointed by the L.C., according to their knowledge of social conditions, work of the courts, consumer affairs and management. They can advise the L.C.

Community Legal Service

- Section 4 requires the Commission to establish and fund a CLS, to secure *individual access to justice*, by providing legal information, advice and help in preventing, settling or resolving disputes and enforcing decisions.
- The section provides that *everyone* involved in the CLS (including lawyers, volunteer advisers and other service providers) should have regard to the desirability of promoting *improvements in the range and quality of services* and of achieving the *swift and fair resolution of disputes*.
- The Commission has a duty to determine the need for and provision of services, *plan what needs to be done* and help other bodies to plan how to meet those needs.
- It can set and *monitor standards* and provide accreditation schemes for service providers. The Commission runs the CLS Fund. It must aim to secure *value for money*. It may fund services by entering into contracts, making grants and loans, establishing bodies to provide services or itself provide services, etc. (s.6). It may provide different services for different areas and the L.C. may direct it to provide particular services.

Funding code

The Commission prepares the Code, subject to the L.C.'s approval, setting out the criteria under which it is prepared to provide services. It can make regulations as to when recipients should contribute to the cost of their legal aid, and s.11 provides that costs ordered against a funded individual should be kept to a reasonable amount, taking into account his resources and making allowances for his clothes, furniture and tools of trade.

Criminal Defence Service

- Under s.12, the Commission must establish a CDS "for the purpose of securing that individuals involved in criminal investigations or criminal proceedings have access to such advice, assistance and representation *as the interests of justice require*" (my emphasis). This test is identical to the merits test for criminal legal aid under the pre-1999 scheme and matches the art. 6 requirement, above. *Trivial cases*, where someone can be expected to represent themselves *will not be funded*.
- The Commission can set up an accreditation and monitoring scheme (and has done so) and can fund such advice and assistance as it considers appropriate, under s.13.
- A represented individual may select any representative to act for him and it may be from a prescribed group (i.e. solicitors with a CDS contract) but he cannot be restricted to representation by a person employed by the Commission or a body maintained by the Commission, such as a public defender. *This freedom of choice is required by art.6.*
- Under s.16, the Commission must prepare a *code of conduct* for its employees and service providers which includes a duty of non-discrimination and duties to the court, etc.
- Under s.17 (as amended by the Criminal Defence Service Act 2006), where anyone is represented in a criminal court, they *may be asked to pay for some or all of their representation*.
- Under Sch.3 of the **1999 Act**, the criminal courts are empowered to grant representation but under the **Criminal Defence Service Act 2006** this power is transferred to the Commission, who administer a means test.

KEY POINT

CONDITIONAL FEE ARRANGEMENTS ("NO WIN NO FEE" CONTRACTS)
Very importantly, and VERY controversially, the 1999 Act extended "no win no fee" private contracts, designed *to serve people who cannot now obtain civil legal aid*, under the Act. Under Pt II, a CFA is defined, in s.58(2)

as "an agreement with a person providing advocacy or litigation services which provides for his fee and expenses, or any part of them, to be payable only in specified circumstances". This means a success fee is paid only if the lawyer wins the case. CFAs are prohibited in criminal proceedings and virtually all family proceedings. Section 29 provides that insurance premiums for policies insuring against the risk of losing the case may be recovered in costs awarded by the court (see more below).

Legal Services Consultative Panel

This panel, appointed by the L.C., has "the duty of assisting [him] in the maintenance and development of standards in the education, training and conduct of persons offering legal services".

MODERNISING JUSTICE: THE POLICY BEHIND THE ACT

In the White Paper of this name, the Government explained it had identified these problems, in the old civil legal aid scheme:

- inadequate access to quality information and consequent poor coordination in services;
- inability to control and target legal aid;
- restrictive practices and cumbersome court procedures; and
- the legal advice sector had grown randomly.

KEY POINT

The paper promised a Community Legal Service, as above, to co-ordinate plans of various funders and *treat the advice sector and advice by lawyers under one budget*. Thus it departed from the pure judicare model that had been in place for half a century.

Legal services would be made more affordable by regulating costs and expanding provision for CFAs.

As for criminal defence services, the Government said weaknesses of the old criminal legal aid system were:

- cost;
- lawyers' pay framework was outdated because of inappropriate financial incentives and a few disproportionately expensive cases;

- the means test was flawed because magistrates' clerks were so bad at administering it and were castigated by the Parliamentary Public Accounts Committee for squandering legal aid money for the previous seven years; and
- the legal aid scheme was highly fragmented.

Fundamental reform was necessary. The CDS would develop more efficient ways of procuring services, through contracts with accredited private-practice lawyers and salaried defenders on the model piloted in Scotland. It would abolish means testing for defendants in the magistrates' courts but target rich defendants.

DEVELOPING THE NEW LEGAL SERVICES MODEL IN PRACTICE

The Government started developing its new system even before publishing *Modernising Justice*. Thirteen Regional Legal Service Committees were established in 1997–98 and published their Assessment of Need for Legal Services by 1999. They identified particular groups suffering from an unmet need: those living in rural areas; the elderly; people with mental health problems; people whose first language was not English; and those appearing before employment tribunals.

The new system for civil cases
The Community Legal Service

In 1999, the Government published a consultation paper detailing how it would develop the CLS, setting out the following.

- People needed basic information and advice on rights and responsibilities, not necessarily to go to court.
- 6,000 professionals (lawyers) and 30,000 volunteers at law centres and other advice centres, such as Citizens' Advice Bureaux, etc. provided this for £250 million per year.
- This was enough money but service was fragmented and uncoordinated.
- Local CLS Partnerships (of lawyers, local authorities, advice bodies and funders) would target funds to local needs.
- A legal services website was being developed. (It is now called Community Legal Advice).

The paper gave case studies demonstrating how difficult it was for people with certain problems to obtain satisfactory advice. The lack of an effective referral network meant people got initial advice and were then sent away so the new legal services network should include lawyers, advice workers, paralegals with specialist knowledge, e.g. Trading Standards Officers, and volunteers in Citizens Advice Bureaux, etc.

The CLS should provide information, advice and assistance, argued the paper. Need for legal service varied geographically. Funders were uncoordinated. Time was wasted by advice agencies demonstrating the quality of their services to their different funders, e.g. one Asian women's group had ten funders and 40 per cent of its manager's time was spent on reporting to them. Quantifying need was difficult. Statistics indicated that unmet need for legal services resulted not from inadequate provision but from "lack of access to appropriate adequate help of adequate quality".

Contracting

The introduction of general civil contracting brought a shift in funding of legal services. Whereas under the old legal aid scheme, any solicitor could apply to give legally-aided services but few non-solicitor agencies could, all providers of legal help must now have a contract with the LSC. To get this, an advice agency or firm of solicitors must demonstrate it satisfies the quality criteria. A provider may have a general civil contract, a family contract if on the family panel, or a controlled work contract, in areas such as immigration, mental health, community care, public law and actions against the police. Every contracted supplier gets regular payments based on reports to the Commission. Their work is peer reviewed. Contractors can call specialist phone lines for help in advising clients. Barristers' chambers may be awarded contracts. As we shall see, the LSC is trying to introduce a deeply unpopular scheme of competitive tendering.

Types of Legal Service

The Funding Code replaced the old civil merits test for legal aid. It provides six levels of service, which may be provided in different ways and may attract different rules of eligibility and remuneration. Details are on the LSC website.

1. Legal help, including advice, starting proceedings, advocacy and, *importantly*, mediation and arbitration.
2. Help at court, including representation.
3. Family help, including negotiation.
4. Legal representation (investigative help or full representation).
5. Family mediation.
6. Such other services as are authorised by the LC.

Legal help, help at court and certain types of representation are classified as controlled work and can only be carried out by lawyers or legal advisers with a general civil contract. These providers are fully responsible for granting and withdrawing help in these cases. (In other words, they help the client to complete the application form and they determine whether the client is eligible.) Funding for most cases requiring representation and approved family help is granted by the Commission.

What can be funded?

Eight categories of service are *excluded*, under Sch.2 of the **1999 Act**.

1.   Personal injury, apart from clinical negligence.
2.   Conveyancing.
3.   Boundary disputes.
4.   Wills.
5.   Trust law.
6.   Defamation.
7.   Company or partnership law.
8.   Other business matters.

The Lord Chancellor sets the priorities for funding, currently **Children Act** proceedings, cases where the client is at real and immediate risk of loss of life or liberty, social welfare, domestic violence and serious cases against public authorities. The Code prioritises cases with a wider public interest and significant human rights cases. Funding is provided for representation before certain tribunals, as it was under the old legal aid scheme, though funding has never been extended to all tribunals, because there has never been sufficient money. Very expensive cases must be referred to a Special Cases Unit. Very controversially, personal injuries, for which legal aid had been available, were removed from the scheme because the Government thought that most of those cases could be funded through conditional fee agreements. Clinical negligence cases and actions against the police for tort remain within the scope of the fund.

Merit criteria

"Help" can only be granted if there is sufficient benefit to the client to justify it. Different criteria apply to other types of service. The Code provides various cost-benefit tests, which usually mean comparing likely cost with likely damages obtainable. The "prospects of success" are evaluated for those clients applying for funded *representation*. This means the likelihood of a successful outcome in the proceedings. Generally, at least a 50 per cent prospect of success is required but funding may be granted to borderline cases if, for example, the case has overwhelming importance to the client, has a wider public interest, is a human rights judicial review, involves housing possession, domestic violence or children.

If a claim is allocated to the small claims track, funding will not be granted, because litigants are meant to be able to represent themselves. (This is why suggestions to raise the small claims track limit are always controversial, such as the suggestion by Jackson L.J. in his 2009 interim report on costs in civil cases, mentioned in the civil procedure chapter). It will also be refused if other complaints systems are available, such as an ombudsman. Controversially, investigative help and representation will be refused if the case is suitable for a private CFA contract, described above and further below.

Financial eligibility limits

These are updated annually. Only people with very low incomes and capital are entitled to fully funded services. Those whose income or capital fall above certain limits have to pay a contribution towards certain (but not all) services, assessed according to their means. The logic behind this is that it encourages people to behave reasonably, as if they were spending their own money.

Conditional fee agreements

Help will not be granted in cases suitable for CFAs. This is enormously controversial (see below). A CFA means, for example, a no-win, no-fee contract or a contract whereby the lawyer gets a higher fee (success fee) if he wins the case. Do not confuse it with a contingency fee agreement, whereby the lawyer takes a percentage of any damages won. CFAs were permitted by the **Courts and Legal Services Act 1990** but widened in scope by the **1999 Act**.

The Criminal Defence Service

The Government established four public defenders' offices but PDs are directly employed by the LSC and this was very controversial. English lawyers have traditionally been hostile to PDs as they consider them insufficiently independent. Clients cannot be forced to accept a PD. See further below. From 2001, all solicitors' firms undertaking publicly-funded criminal defence work had to have a contract with the CDS. In July 2000, the L.C. announced he would reduce fees for criminal defence lawyers, to reduce the disparity between fees paid to prosecutors and defence lawyers. As described below, the system of paying lawyers may soon change radically, following Lord Carter's 2006 Review.

MORE BACKGROUND: WHY WAS THE OLD LEGAL AID SCHEME SCRAPPED?

- Throughout the 1990s, both the Conservative Government then its Labour successor were seriously concerned that something radical had to be done to reform the provision of legal services. Why?
- The cost was "spiralling out of control", according to the Conservative Lord Chancellor, Lord Mackay. Legal aid was the only demand-led draw on the Treasury. Some years in the 1990s, the cost rose by around 20 per cent, despite the fact that fewer people were being legally aided. The **Children Act 1989**, providing separate representation for children, and the development of duty solicitor schemes in police stations and the magistrates' courts accelerated the cost increase and the media became concerned that a few cases cost millions of pounds, and in come cases apparently wealthy defendants were legally aided.
- *Unmet legal need* was identified by research in the 1970s. It means that where someone has a problem which could be remedied by use of the law, that problem remains unsolved through lack of legal help. It was (and is) caused by:

  - the high cost of legal fees;
  - fear of lawyers, fear of cost;
  - lawyers' lack of training and unwillingness to serve poor clients' needs for advice in welfare law;
  - the inaccessibility of lawyers' offices to poor or rural clients;
  - the creation of new legal rights without the funding to enforce them;
  - people's ignorance that the law could solve their problem; and
  - the fact that the legal aid scheme omitted certain services, such as representation at tribunals.

- Funders were uncoordinated. Legal aid was designed to deliver legal services through the medium of private practice barristers and solicitors so alternative legal services, listed below, received very little of the huge budget and were dependent on a precarious mix of sources, such as charities, local authorities and other government departments.
- Criminal legal aid was administered unevenly. Research showed that the "Widgery criteria" merits test was applied differently between magistrates' courts, and the Audit Commission criticised them eight years running for failing to apply the means test properly. "Fat cat lawyers", as Lord Irvine L.C. called them, were charging the Legal Aid Board exorbitant fees.
- In 1999, Hazel Genn published a survey of how people solved their legal problems: *Paths to Justice*, summarised at (1999) 149 N.L.J. 1756. She

found that people were generally extraordinarily ignorant about their legal rights and obligations.

"Alternative" legal services

Because the shortcomings of the legal aid scheme and the causes of unmet legal need were identified from the 1970s, alternatives to legal aid delivered by private-practice lawyers were developed to try to meet that need. These can no longer be seen as alternatives because they have been absorbed into mainstream state-funded legal services.

- *Law Centres* were deliberately established in poor areas, with a user-friendly shop front image, where employed lawyers and paralegals provided advice and representation on such matters as welfare law and immigration. They have existed since 1973 but have always suffered from vulnerable funding. Those financed by local authorities found they were biting the hand that fed them, when they acted for groups suffering bad public housing. Law centre funding was (and is) unpredictable and unreliable and sometimes they close temporarily.

- Favoured by the Rushcliffe Committee then Thatcher from 1979, *Citizens Advice Bureaux* now use 20,000 volunteers, advising at over 3,000 locations. They are grossly overstretched, as a 2009 *Times* report disclosed.

- 800 independent *advice centres*, covering diverse areas, sometimes provide legal representation themselves, or make referrals. Examples are the Child Poverty Action Group, Shelter, Youth Access, The Money Advice Trust, Dial UK (disability advice), Mind, the Refugee Legal Centre, etc. Lawyers often provide advice free at evening advice centres but need to make a referral if substantive legal help is needed.

- *Pro bono* groups of solicitors and barristers, where professionals pledge to give their services free to some clients. The Free Representation Unit, a group of Bar students prepared to represent claimants in appearances before tribunals, etc. was established in 1972.

- In addition, Governments from the 1980s have promoted various other ways of helping people solve their legal problems, to save public money:

  - Helping people represent themselves by simplifying procedure (plain English Civil Procedure Rules, explained in the civil procedure chapter) and providing good advice leaflets and websites.
  - Encouraging ADR, the cheaper and quicker resolution of disputes, out of court (see civil procedure chapter).
  - Encouraging private legal expenses insurance.

- Asking government departments to explain their decisions better and provide accessible complaints mechanisms, like ombudsmen.

DEVELOPMENTS SINCE 2000 AND EVALUATION OF THE CURRENT LEGAL SERVICES SCHEME

Flexibility
In one sense, the scheme was quite visionary. Labour had the simple idea of finding out how much money was spent on legal aid and alternative legal services and working out the level and nature of local legal needs and how they could best be fulfilled, whether through private-practice lawyers or alternatives and thus abandoning the *judicare* model which presumed people could only get legal services from a barrister or solicitor. The new scheme enabled the Legal Services Fund to be used in a more imaginative manner. Lord Irvine L.C. extended funded representation to more systems of tribunal and to inquests into deaths in custody. Public interest cases can now be funded, even if they are in categories normally ineligible, such as an appeal to the law lords to clarify the nature of the duty owed by drivers of police vehicles answering an emergency call, and a multi-party action of claims arising out of police action at a May Day protest. Contracts were granted for telephone advice lines and "outreach" work (advice services provided at alternative venues such as doctors' surgeries or libraries). Contracts covered debt, immigration, welfare benefits, education and housing. More contracts were granted for such innovations as a virtual law centre and community outreach projects for old people, young people, women in rural areas, and so on. Hundreds of courts were given CLS quality marks as information points.

Community Legal Services Partnerships
These were praised, by research, as a forum for sharing ideas, but the Law Society and the Legal Action Group complained that they cost a lot to administer but lacked the funds to apply their ideas.

Private practice
Barristers and solicitors in private practice still provide 92 per cent of civil legal services contracts, thus the model of delivery has not changed much.

Public defenders
A 2002 LSC report on the four public defender pilot schemes found them to be a "considerable success" after the first year and their numbers were increased to eight, but this is nothing compared with the thousands of solicitors' firms with

CDS contracts. In 2007, Bridges and others published research showing that PDs gave high quality services but were more expensive than private practice. By 2008, four of the eight PD offices closed, as they were not cost effective.

Advice deserts—unmet legal need got worse

By 2003, the new system attracted widespread criticism because the availability of civil legal help via solicitors had radically decreased in some areas, without the provision of alternatives. The Law Society and other groups such as the Legal Action Group expressed serious concern that so many solicitors' firms had withdrawn from the legal services scheme that there were *advice deserts*, such as Kent, where there were no solicitors doing funded housing law. In *Geography of Advice* (2004) Citizens Advice reported a "postcode lottery". Forty per cent of their Bureaux operated in advice deserts. Unmet need persisted. The LSC estimated that two million people a year had a significant problem but failed to obtain advice. In 2003, the Commission provided £4.7 million for community legal advice initiatives, mostly education, such as domestic violence awareness and debt prevention. Nevertheless, the Law Society and the Legal Action Group were concerned that the Government had not enhanced access to justice enough to reduce social exclusion, as it had promised. A 2003–04 survey by the Legal Services Research Centre of the Legal Services Commission, *Causes of Action: Civil Law and Social Justice*, by Pleasance and others found that one third of adults had experienced a civil law problem in the previous 3.5 years. About a million problems a year were left unsolved as people did not understand their basic rights. About 37 per cent of people chose to handle their problems alone. Socially excluded groups were especially vulnerable. Civil justice problems often occurred in clusters, such as personal injury causing loss of home or income. Fifteen per cent of those who sought advice did not obtain any, especially over homelessness, rented housing, anti-social neighbours or benefits. The more advisers a person was referred to, the less likely they were to follow up those referrals. The LSC responded by increasing telephone and online advice and establishing more outreach advice clinics in isolated regions and for specific groups.

Poor remuneration

Solicitors and barristers have increasingly complained of poor remuneration for publicly funded work, resulting in many of them abandoning it. A Law Society survey in 2003 found that 90 per cent of respondent solicitors were dissatisfied with the system, citing poor pay, excessive bureaucracy and audits (checks on their work). Seventy-eight per cent threatened to drop or reduce publicly funded work. Junior barristers are paid derisory amounts for simple matters in the Crown Court. At the time of writing, solicitors' and barristers' complaints have accelerated, thanks to the Carter proposals, below.

The cost remains problematic

Because the new system scrapped the means test for criminal defence in the magistrates' courts, the consequent expense of providing criminal defence meant a reduction in civil legal aid. When Lord Carter was asked to report on restructuring the remuneration system, in 2005, it was because the cost of criminal legal aid had risen by 37 per cent in the previous eight years and spending on civil legal aid had been reduced by 24 per cent. The CDS overspent by £60 million in 2002. This was caused by the Government's "crackdown" on crime and the need to advise asylum seekers. The cost of "very high cost" criminal cases rose. There were repeated complaints of the high amounts paid to Q.C.s ("fat cats") in such cases. The Serious Fraud Office prosecuted more complex frauds and the Blair Government had created 360 new criminal offences between 1997–2004 without any increase in the legal aid budget to pay for its new crime initiatives. Ultimately, the response to the problem of the criminal aid budget plundering the civil aid budget was to reintroduce means testing for criminal defence in magistrates' courts. This was reintroduced by the **Criminal Defence Service Act 2006**. This was claimed to have saved £35 million a year. Reintroducing means testing was proposed in the Crown Court in 2009. Acquitted defendants would get their contributions back. By 2005, the UK had the largest legal aid budget in the developed world. Nevertheless, the Legal Action Group pointed out that this only represented 0.4 per cent of public spending. The cost per civil case rose, despite fewer people receiving civil aid. By 2004, 80 per cent of the civil budget was absorbed by family cases. In their own 2005 review, the Government acknowledged that criminal legal aid costs had risen 37 per cent in real terms in seven years, while spending on civil and family cases, excluding asylum, had fallen by 24 per cent. Spending on advocates had risen since 1999 by 20 per cent above inflation. In 2009, the LSC said the average cost of a family case had increased 134 per cent over five years.

Law Centres

The number rose after the **1999 Act** but they continue to be vulnerable to withdrawal of their funding. See L.C. Federation website.

Conditional fee agreements

Private CFAs with solicitors were meant to provide access to justice for those clients for whom legal aid was scrapped, such as claimants in personal injury cases. When this proposal was announced in 1998, lawyers bitterly attacked the Labour Lord Chancellor, Lord Irvine, for threatening to get rid of most civil legal aid and replace it with CFAs and, as can be seen above, legal services will not be granted where the client can be expected to negotiate a CFA. Research by Yarrow, summarised at (2001) 151 N.L.J. 750 revealed that solicitors were using CFAs to overcharge. Case law demonstrated extreme confusion over who should pay success fees and the insurance premiums attached to CFAs and the mess had to be sorted out by the CA in *Callery v Gray* [2001] EWCA Civ 1117. Many lawyers and judges consider some clients are now completely denied access to justice. Research by Stoy Hayward in 2001 confirmed this by suggesting that firms "cherry picked" the cases most likely to succeed and this was confirmed by a damning report in 2004 by Citizens Advice. Injured persons with low value or equivocal cases were left without a remedy. There was no system for regulating the quality and cost of advice. Consumers, such as accident victims in hospital, were subjected to high pressure sales tactics. Consumers were not clear of the risks they took, not understanding that they might have to pay an insurance premium against losing the case and this would deplete the damages they won. On the other hand, some solicitors argue that CFAs have opened up access to justice for people with problems such as defamation claims that were (and are) excluded from legal aid.

Critical reviews

Several reviews were published in 2004 and they made some calls for fundamental reform or restructuring of the system.

1. The Law Society, in *Protecting Rights and Tackling Social Exclusion* urged that the budgets for civil and criminal aid should be separated and the Government should develop public legal education. Government departments should acknowledge the demands they created on the legal aid budget. ADR should be promoted.
2. The Parliamentary Constitutional Affairs Select Committee produced two reports in 2003–04. It criticised legal aid deserts and persistent unmet need, complaining that only the poorest people were served and people of modest means were denied access to justice. It recommended that spending on criminal legal aid should be curbed. It criticised auditing of contracted providers as wasteful and suggested peer review instead. Over-specialisation prevented a holistic approach by solicitors.
3. *The Independent Review of the Community Legal Service* said the CLS lacked an evidence base to demonstrate how it tackled social exclusion. Contracting and quality assurance were unduly bureaucratic.

60th Anniversary Review

To read intelligent analysis and critique, go to the Legal Action Group website and click on "Magazine". This gives the editorials from *Legal Action* and lots of useful articles. In 2009, LAG published *The Justice Gap*, to coincide with the 60th anniversary of legal aid. They argue that legal aid has fallen short of its original aims and there is "a marked difference between the numbers of cases pursued to enforce rights and the many potential cases that people never take up as they are either not aware of their rights or they decide it is not worth the trouble to take it further—this is 'the justice gap' ". For example, they observed county court housing repossession cases, where "traumatised" people were subject to proceedings from their mortgage lenders and making last-minute negotiations, unsure of what was going on and ill-informed. LAG's Jon Robins also wrote an article in the *New law Journal*, complaining of the lack of legal aid in tribunals. He said only seven per cent of families of personnel killed in Afghanistan or Iraq received legal aid for representation at the inquests: (2009) 159 N.L.J. 131. LAG are concerned at the decline in the not-for-profit sector of legal service providers.

Government response to criticism

From 2003, the Government started shifting policy from the much criticised audit system to peer review. After criticism that there were too many suppliers touting for business amongst asylum seekers, it limited suppliers in this field and introduced salaried solicitors and case workers. After consultation in 2005, it announced cuts.

- Eligibility for representation would be cut, in an attempt to encourage early dispute settlement. Eligibility for help (instead) would be increased.
- Family services would be restructured to encourage early out-of-court settlement. Unreasonable conduct would be deterred in family cases. Multiple and repeat applications in private law family cases would be curbed.
- In clinical disputes (e.g. against hospitals) and actions against the police, the LSC would be expected to take account of whether the applicant had exhausted all complaints mechanisms.
- Restrictions might be introduced on very high cost civil cases.

In 2005, the Government produced a consultation paper, *Making Legal Rights a Reality*, publishing the results in 2006. It acknowledged the crisis in civil legal advice, caused by a drop in funding of 22 per cent since 1997. The new strategy recognised the need to provide holistic services (to tackle all the client's potential civil problems). It proposed working with local authorities to establish 75 Community Legal Advice Centres (CLACs) and Networks to "provide access to a service which ranges from basic advice to legal representation in the full range of social welfare problems as well as children and family legal problems". Contracts would be awarded after a tendering process. Alarmingly, it threatened to withdraw funding from the Law Centres Federation but that proposal has now been dropped. The Federation's director, Steve Hynes, commented that CLACs sound just like law centres and wondered why there was a need to establish a new "brand". He reported that two CLACs had been announced in Gateshead and Leicester. He criticised this, because they already had long-established law centres. See his Comment, "Risky rebranding?" (2006) 156 N.L.J. 657. The Government published the results of their review in 2005, *A Fairer Deal for Legal Aid*, saying they would reform the management of large, complex cases, reduce spending on high cost criminal cases and improve the way fraud cases were brought to justice.

LORD CARTER'S REVIEW OF LEGAL AID PROCUREMENT

In 2005, the Government established Lord Carter's Review of legal aid procurement to take the heat out of the argument between them and legal aid practitioners about proposed cuts in lawyers' remuneration. He reported in 2006: *Legal Aid: a Market-Based Approach to Reform*, recommending:

- "best value" tendering for legal aid contracts;
- responsibilities for Law Society and Bar Council to enhance the quality of the legal aid supplier market;
- fixed fees for solicitors carrying out legal aid work in police stations;
- revised graduated fees for Crown Court advocates;
- a new graduated fee scheme for Crown Court litigators to reward earlier preparation and resolution of cases;
- tighter control of very high cost criminal legal aid cases;
- standard fees for civil and family legal help; and
- new graduated fees for solicitors in private law family and child care proceedings.

Responses to Carter
- Research commissioned by the Law Society suggested that 800 solicitors' firms will cease to deliver criminal defence. Critics fear black and minority ethnic (BME) solicitors will be squeezed out, because many of them are sole practitioners or in small firms.
- A defender of the proposals, Keogh, at (2006) 156 N.L.J. 1149, pointed out that Carter found the UK spends 10 times more on criminal defence than its nearest rival, with no obvious explanation.
- See, however, condemnatory comment by S. Willman (2006) 156 N.L.J. 1537 and other negative comments at p.1541.

2009 plans to implement Carter—and reactions
In a 2009 paper, *Legal Aid: Funding Reforms*, the Government proposed reducing and fixing expert witness rates, cutting fees for criminal defence work

(defence advocates currently get 23 per cent more than prosecutors), introducing best value tendering for police station work and reintroducing means testing in criminal Crown Court cases, as above. At the same time, the LSC proposed fixed fees in family cases, worth a 20 per cent cut in hourly rate for barristers and, according to the Law Society, resulting in nine tenths of family solicitors losing income. The Government's rationale was to spend more on *civil* legal services. In 2009, they raised the civil eligibility limit by five per cent so more people were aided and they boosted funds for "not-for-profit" agencies from £24 million in 2001–02 to £80 million. Naturally this provoked widespread opposition from criminal and family lawyers. See three pages from F. Gibb in the *Times*, July 17, 2009 and many comments in law journals, such as the N.L.J., from July 2009. Family lawyers said their system was at breaking point and criminal lawyers said there would be more miscarriages of justice, as more inexperienced lawyers took on criminal defence work. They criticised the proposal that privately funded clients would not get all their costs back, saying this breached the presumption of innocence.

By the time of writing, October 2009, very little progress has been made on Carter's proposals because naturally lawyers oppose them so strongly. To expect otherwise would be to imagine turkeys would vote for Christmas.

Revision Checklist

You should now know and understand:

- the defects of the pre-1999 legal aid scheme;
- the current model under the 1999 Act;
- the reasoning behind it;
- its defects; and
- proposals to adjust the current model, following the Carter Review and consequent criticisms.

FURTHER READING/UPDATING

Darbyshire on the ELS, 2008, Chapter 17, further reading therein and website updates
Law Society's *Gazette* (free, online)
Legal Action (some parts free on the LAG website)
New Law Journal

Websites (the last two are the most useful)
Bar Council
Carter Review
CLS Direct
Law Centres Federation
Law Society and Law Society's Gazette
Legal Action Group
Legal Services Commission

QUESTION AND ANSWER

The Question

Outline and evaluate the current legal services scheme.

Advice and the Answer

Advice

There is ample information in this chapter to answer the question because all that is really needed is an intelligent and balanced summary of some of the sections above.

Answer guidelines

1. Outline the present scheme under the **Access to Justice Act 1999.**
2. Explain the reasoning behind it (spiralling cost, limitations of legal aid).
3. Examine the criticisms of its shortcomings and the government's responses, including backtracking on some policies such as the means test for criminal legal aid.
4. Comment on the fact that though it was designed to open up and expand the range of providers in the not-for-profit sector, over 90 per cent of publicly funded legal services are still provided by private practice lawyers so the judicare model is still pre-eminent.
5. Think about and comment on the problem of providing adequate help for people with legal problems. Are some of these problems insoluble?

Handy Hints and Useful Websites

12

ESSAYS

Identify what is required to answer the question

There are likely to be several elements, each of which requires a response. Do not ignore any element, or you may lose substantial marks or fail. Make sure you have identified what is required of you. It may be fruitful to check with fellow students that you have correctly identified what is required of you, though of course the work that you produce for assessment must be entirely your own.

Research

1. Start by reading the relevant chapters in the core course books that your lecturers/tutors have recommended.
2. In an undergraduate ELS essay, it is highly unlikely that you will be able to answer a question by using only a textbook. Examine any further reading that appears to be relevant, that your lecturers/tutors have recommended, or that is referred to in your course text.
3. Examine any electronic or hard copy documents referred to or obviously related to the question or issue that you are researching.
4. Examine legal websites and databases, such as those listed below and in the chapters above. You may wish to download documents and save them to your own computer to read on screen rather than printing them out, which is expensive.
5. Do not start with an aimless Google search and do not even think about citing Wikipedia or similar websites in preference to your textbooks. Use a law dictionary or encyclopaedia such as *Halsbury*, which you can access electronically if you are a university student.
6. Note that this subject changes so rapidly that you need to appreciate that the law, the issues and the circumstances may have changed since the sources you are using were published, including this book. The websites listed here will help you to update the information you have. It is worth checking the press releases archived on the relevant websites and the free updates on *Darbyshire on the ELS* (2008) on Sweet & Maxwell's website.

7. Make accurate notes about the sources of your information including an accurate reference so that you can footnote your sources properly and compile your bibliography.
8. If you are working from your own photocopies, printouts or books, then highlighting is much quicker than taking notes.

Content

Address the terms of the question. This is the most crucial part of the assessment. Those grading your work need to see that you have understood the task and taken the correct approach, so do not "write all you know". You will be assessed on your:

*   ability to identify the legal and policy issues raised by the question or problem;
*   knowledge of relevant law;
*   knowledge and understanding of policy issues, where relevant, including proposals for reform and background to the law;
*   ability to conduct careful, thorough, relevant and accurate research; and
*   insight into and thoughtful approach to the issues.

"Discuss"   means more than just describe the law or topic. It means explain the issues surrounding the topic and address them. For instance, if it is a legal change you are asked to discuss, look at the background to the change in the law. If it is a controversial issue you are asked to discuss, look at the "pros and cons" of the plans, as articulated by Government critics and defenders.

"Critically discuss" or "critically evaluate"   does not mean you have to say something bad about the topic. The word "criticism" is used in the sense of theatre criticism. You should look at the pros and cons of the issue, citing relevant sources and, if possible, forming your own opinion. Every *Sun* reader has an opinion on elements of the ELS, such as the jury, but you are expected to develop a well-informed opinion.

Structure   Ensure that there is a clear thread of argument running through your essay. Sub-headings may help you to organise the material and will provide "signposts" to the reader. If you form an opinion, make sure that you acknowledge that there may be different opinions on the subject and briefly address those different opinions.

Write a straightforward introduction and conclusion. It will be easiest to write the introduction once you have written the body of the essay. Be as brief as possible. Your introduction should be no more than a very short paragraph.

Expression, style and mechanics

Write in a style which is clear and fluent. Use short sentences. The longer your sentences and the more pretentious your language, the more likely you are to get into trouble.

Be very concise. Stick to the word limit. You should read through every sentence many times, ensuring that you have expressed yourself in as few words as possible and not repeated yourself. Waffle is your enemy.

Carefully proof read your work several times to avoid typographical and other technical errors.

List the material you have used in a bibliography and footnote your citations, making sure that you do not abuse footnotes by making substantive points that ought to have been made in the text.

Immaculate use of language is an essential tool of the lawyer's trade

Use of grammar and punctuation affects the meaning of the law and the meaning and quality of your work. Clumsily expressed work with bad grammar and spelling mistakes detracts enormously from the substance of what you are saying. Use a dictionary or a thesaurus but do not forget that the spellchecker on your computer must be set to English (UK). If possible, ask someone to read through your work.

Mistakes of English commonly found in law students' essays

1. Do not use slang and elisions (don't, won't, can't, etc.). You must write in formal English.
2. Capitals: pay attention to your textbooks to find out what words need to begin with a capital. For instance, Parliament and the present Government begin with a capital but not when referring to governments in general. There is one single High Court and one Crown Court but many magistrates' courts and county courts. Nouns in general do not need a capital but titles do.
3. Sentence structure: students commonly use clauses as sentences. Sentences always contain a subject and a verb.
4. "However" is not a conjunction. It cannot be used in a place where "and", "but" or "so" can be used. It should not appear at the beginning of a sentence. Shift it into the sentence and place a comma either side, e.g. "The Government, however, decided not to follow this recommendation".
5. The Grocer's "s": "Cabbage's on special offer today". In this sentence, "cabbages" does not need an apostrophe "s". The word is the plural of "cabbage". "The judge's robes" is a phrase requiring an apostrophe "s" to represent the possessive case and means "the robes of the judge".
6. Paragraphing: choose one type of paragraph break, either an indentation or a line space. Do not mix the two.

Help with English

Around half of first year undergraduates produce essays demonstrating weak use of English, especially those educated in England. Immaculate use of English is not only essential for obtaining a good grade in undergraduate assessments, it is also an essential transferable skill. Learning English is a lifelong task for all of us, including those of us who write professionally. These guides may help. Check for the latest edition.

J. Clancy, *How to Write Essays*

J. Cochrane and J. Humphrys, *Between You and I: A Little Book of Bad English*

D. Collinson, *Plain English*

R.R. Jordan, *Academic Writing*

R. Lawrence, *The Penguin Guide to Punctuation*

G. Leech, *An A-Z of English Grammar*

R. Marius, *A Writer's Companion*

A. Northedge, *The Good Study Guide*

R. Palmer, *Write in Style*

J. Peck, *The Student's Guide to Writing*

M. Swan, *Practical English Usage*

M. Swan, *How English Works*

R. Task, *Penguin Guide to Punctuation*

J. Trezrciak & S. Mackay, *Study Skills for Academic Writing*

L. Truss, *Eats, Shoots and Leaves: the Zero Tolerance Approach to Punctuation*

M. Vince, *Advanced Language Practice*

D. Watson, *Advanced Vocabulary in Context*

Dyslexia

If you are dyslexic, or think you may be, seek out the help of the dyslexia unit at your university. Remember to ensure that lecturers or tutors marking your work know that you are a dyslexic.

Plagiarism

Plagiarism is a form of cheating. It means copying someone else's work or ideas and passing them off as your own. If you join with a friend in preparing coursework, make sure the end product is all your own. Do not copy from one another. You may use a large number of sources, such as books, articles and websites but all must be meticulously cited. You will frequently use secondary sources, such as text-books. Again, you must point this out. For instance, if you find a useful article or book, quoted in a textbook or another article, then footnote it as *"Fletcher, Rethinking Criminal Law*, as cited in Smith and Hogan's *Criminal Law*, at p.103".

EXAM CHECKLIST

Revision: how?

Start early, otherwise you may waste the summer (or all next year!) revising for a resit. Draw up a revision timetable and stick to it. You will underestimate the time taken to revise. If your lecture notes and others are scrappy, you may find it helpful to make revision notes. Visit the Memory section of the BBC website for a programme containing tips on how to improve your memory http://www.bbc.co.uk/radio4/memory/

Revision: what?

1. You should aim to know your whole course fairly well and as much of it as possible in greater depth. Question spotting is very difficult in ELS, as there can be so many different permutations of topics, e.g. "the adversarial process" includes civil and criminal trial and pre-trial; legal profession might be combined with judiciary or with legal services, etc. It helps, however, to know your own course. Know the topics your course teachers have emphasised in your year. Topicality means past papers are, in some respects, unhelpful. Do not revise from notes for other courses and do not fool yourself that this *Nutshell* is anything but a revision aid, a comforter. It is not a substitute for having worked hard and read widely, throughout the year. Beware that it may omit things emphasised in your course, e.g. police powers.

2. Know the approach of your course, as well as its content. Most ELS courses are analytical and discursive, much more so than this *Nutshell*, but the ability to appreciate ELS in the context of this approach comes from wide reading. ELS for undergraduates in non-law courses and students on other courses is usually much more factual, and takes a "tools for the trade" approach.

3. This is the most fast changing area of law. Have you made sure that the information you have been revising is totally up to date? This book was proof read in autumn 2009. Have things changed since then?

4. Have you familiarised yourself with critiques of various elements of the system? Look out for those which have appeared since October 2009. Especially good sources of brief, pithy articles and editorials are the *New Law Journal* and *Legal Action*. Do not forget *The Times* law reports are another great source of brand new case law.

5. Read all the newest consultation papers on the MoJ website and find out what the responses were and whether there were any outcomes in changes of law or practice.

In the exam
Organise your time

Every year I groan over a handful of 2A students who achieve thirds or fails because they have answered two and a half or three questions instead of four. Think about it. If you answer three instead of four, you must achieve an average of 66 per cent in those three, just to attain an examination mark of 50 per cent (just a 2B). Divide the exam time by the number of answers required and force yourself to move on when time is up. Leave ample space between answers to add points, even in neat note form, to your earlier answers, if you can spare 10 minutes at the end. Lecturers always say, and some students never seem to understand the simple point, that it is much easier to gain 30 marks on answering a new question than to add 30 to a near-complete one. Do not waffle. Write clearly. Try rollerball or superior ballpoint. See which is quicker and neater. Fountain pens are too slow. Bad writing is bound to affect the markers, as they cannot get the "gist", the "flow" of an argument, even if they can slowly interpret it, word by word. If your handwriting is bad, get help urgently, in college or privately. If English is not your first language, practise it by getting as much of your written English checked as you can persuade people to mark (on any topic). Again, if you need remedial help, your college may provide it. In the exam, you need time for mental translation. Time will be your enemy so make every word count. Waffle is even more dangerous for you than for a native student.

Answer the question set

If you panic and misread a question on juries as one on magistrates, you may get 0. If you "write all you know" where a critical analysis or a particular approach is needed, you may just scrape a pass, if you are lucky. Plan your answer and only include that which is required. Do not be tempted to demonstrate knowledge just because you have revised it.

Be authoritative

The trouble with this subject is that every *Sun* reader has an opinion on the jury or the legal profession. You must substantiate your beliefs with fact and authoritative opinion. Most opinions have found written expression in some text, article or committee report, sometimes in many, but do not invent sources/quotations. Your examiner will know better. Being authoritative comes from wide reading, not a *Nutshell*. Be original: very difficult but the more so the better. Reach your own informed opinions. Draw on your own observation of courts and tribunals. They provide hours of free entertainment on a wet Wednesday afternoon. Read a quality newspaper daily. Search for new commentaries and articles in law journals.

ENGLISH LEGAL SYSTEM WEBSITES

Administrative Justice & Tribunals Council http://www.ajtc.gov.uk/
Attorney General http://www.attorneygeneral.gov.uk/
Bar Council www.barcouncil.org.uk
British and Irish Legal Information Institute http://www.bailii.org/
Central Office of Information http://www.coi.gov.uk/
Centre for Effective Dispute Resolution (ADR) http://www.cedr.co.uk/
Community Legal Service http://www.clsdirect.org.uk/index.jsp
Criminal Cases Review Commission www.ccrc.gov.uk
Criminal Courts Review www.criminal-courts-review.org.uk
Criminal Justice System http://www.cjsonline.org/index.html
Crown Prosecution Service www.cps.gov.uk
Department for Constitutional Affairs, now replaced by the Ministry of Justice.
Archived material to mid-2007 is very useful http://www.dca.gov.uk
European Court of Human Rights http://www.echr.coe.int/echr
EC and EU institutions and EC documents, including European Commission and
European Court of Justice http://europa.eu/
European Commission Representation in the UK, for EU news, publications,
info and free email newsletter http://ec.europa.eu/unitedkingdom/
UK Government information http://www.direct.gov.uk/Homepage/fs/en
Her Majesty's Courts Service http://www.hmcourts-service.gov.uk/
Home Office www.homeoffice.gov.uk
International Courts of Justice are best accessed via the UN website
http://www.un.org/
Judiciary http://www.judiciary.gov.uk/
Judicial Appointments Commission http://www.judicialappointments.gov.uk/
Judicial Studies Board http://www.jsboard.co.uk/
Law Commission http://www.lawcom.gov.uk/
Lawlinks, run by the University of Kent at Canterbury: http://library.kent.ac.uk/
library/lawlinks/
Law Society http://www.lawsociety.org.uk/home.law
Law Society's *Gazette*: http://www.lawgazette.co.uk/home.law
Legal Abbreviations, contains 12,500 abbreviations http://www.legalabbrevs.
cardiff.ac.uk/
Legal Action Group www.lag.org.uk
Legal Services Commission www.legalservices.gov.uk
Legal Services Research Centre: www.lsrc.org.uk
Lexis is a very comprehensive database. Access it via your library's e-resources.
Liberty www.liberty-human-rights.org.uk
Ministry of Justice http://www.justice.gov.uk/
National Assembly for Wales http://www.assemblywales.org/index.htm

Office of Public Sector Information, including Acts of Parliament and statutory instruments http://www.opsi.gov.uk/

Parliament www.parliament.uk

Privy Council Judicial Committee www.privy-council.org.uk

Scottish Parliament: www.scottish.parliament.uk

The Times http://www.timesonline.co.uk

UK Newsstand, all UK newspapers is available via your library's e-resources.

UK Supreme Court http://www.supremecourt.gov.uk/index.html

US Supreme Court www.supremecourtus.gov

Westlaw, another very comprehensive subscriber database, containing all case law, statute law many law journals and accessed via library e-resources

Index

LEGAL TAXONOMY
FROM SWEET & MAXWELL

This index has been prepared using Sweet and Maxwell's Legal Taxonomy. Main index entries conform to keywords provided by the Legal Taxonomy except where references to specific documents or non-standard terms (denoted by quotation marks) have been included. These keywords provide a means of identifying similar concepts in other Sweet & Maxwell publications and online services to which keywords from the Legal Taxonomy have been applied. Readers may find some minor differences between terms used in the text and those which appear in the index.

Suggestions to **sweetandmaxwell.taxonomy@thomson.com**.